ABOUT THE AUTHOR

Steve MacDonogh was born in Dublin and has lived since 1982 in the
Dingle area. His previous books include a folklore study, *Green and
Gold: The Wrenboys of Dingle*, and three collections of poetry. He is also
editor of *The Brandon Book of Irish Short Stories*, and his publishing auto-
biography, *Open Book: One Publisher's War*, was published in 1999. A
former chairperson of the Irish Writers' Co-operative and former presi-
dent of the Irish Book Publishers' Association, CLÉ, he is the publisher
at Brandon and Mount Eagle Publications.

Publishers' Note

Every care has been taken to ensure the accuracy of information contained in this book. However, Mount Eagle Publications Ltd cannot accept responsibility for errors or omissions, but if such are brought to their attention future editions will be amended accordingly. Also, information which is correct at the date of publication may become outdated or incorrect.

The publishers wish to thank the advertisers for their support; advertisements have not, however, been allowed to influence editorial content.

THE
DINGLE
PENINSULA

Steve MacDonogh

Illustrated with photographs by Steve MacDonogh
and maps by Jack Roberts and Justin May

This colour edition first published in 2000 by
Brandon
an imprint of Mount Eagle Publications Ltd
Dingle, Co. Kerry, Ireland.

Text © Steve MacDonogh 1993, 2000

Photographs © Steve MacDonogh 2000

Maps of the Dingle Way by Justin May © Cork Kerry Tourism 1992; based on the
Ordnance Survey by permission of the Government (Permit No. 5542)

Maps of the Dingle peninsula by Jack Roberts © Brandon Book Publishers Ltd 1993
and Mount Eagle Publications Ltd 2000; based on the Ordnance Survey by permission
of the Government

Seamus Heaney's "In Gallarus Oratory" (*Door Into the Dark*: 1969) is reproduced by
permission of Faber and Faber; "Pity the Islanders, *Lucht an Oileáin*" is reproduced by
permission of David Quin

ISBN 0 86322 269 2

Cover design: id communications, Tralee
Cover photographs: Steve MacDonogh
Typeset by Brandon and Red Barn
Printed by CraftPrint

CONTENTS

LIST OF ILLUSTRATIONS

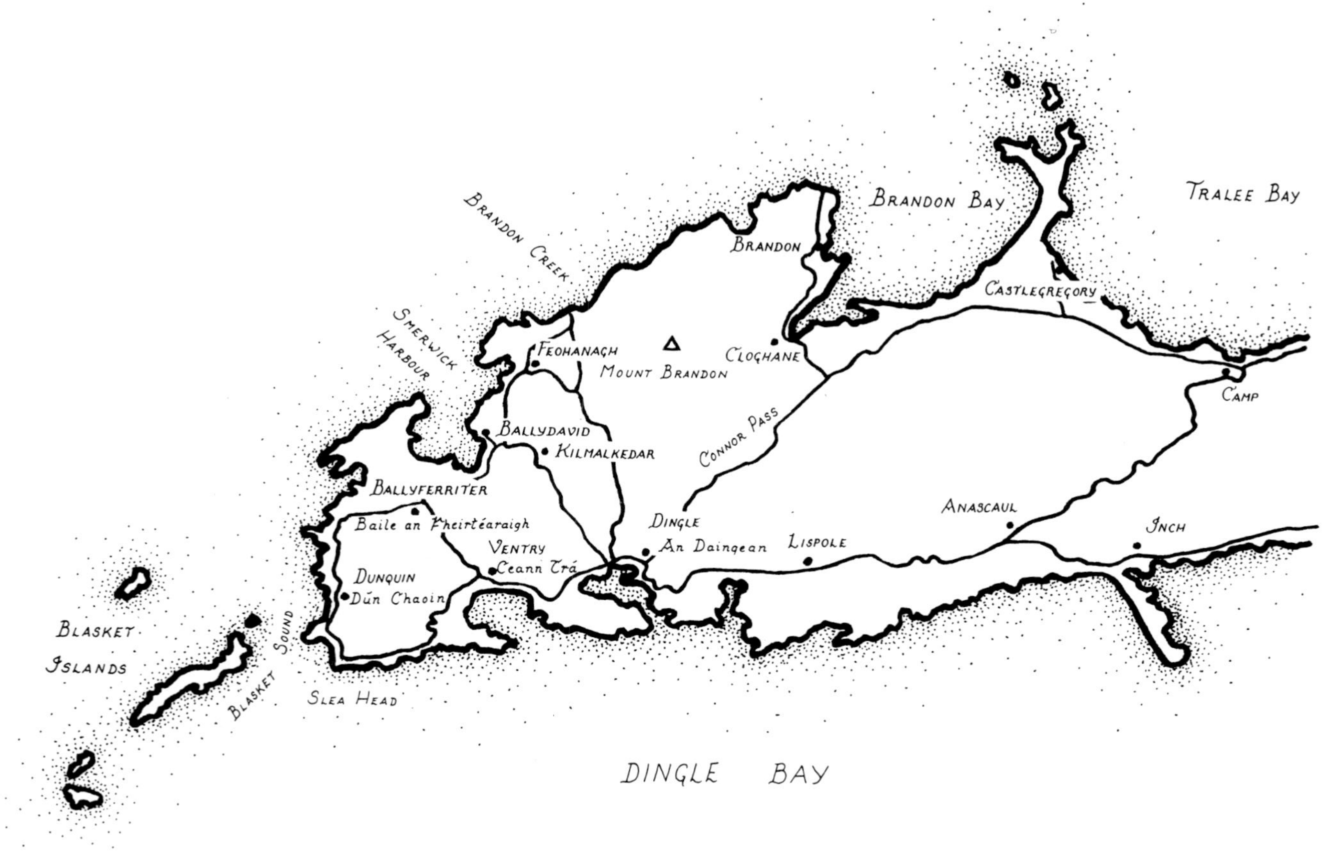

TRALEE BAY
BRANDON BAY
BRANDON CREEK
BRANDON
CASTLEGREGORY
SMERWICK HARBOUR
FEOHANAGH
MOUNT BRANDON
CLOGHANE
CAMP
BALLYDAVID
KILMALKEDAR
CONNOR PASS
BALLYFERRITER
Baile an Fheirtéaraigh
DINGLE
An Daingean
LISPOLE
ANASCAUL
INCH
VENTRY
Ceann Trá
DUNQUIN
Dún Chaoin
BLASKET ISLANDS
BLASKET SOUND
SLEA HEAD
DINGLE BAY

INTRODUCTION

DINGLE IS ONE of the most favoured spots in Ireland for the independently minded visitor. The *National Geographic Traveler* has described it as "the most beautiful place on earth". Bounded on three sides by the sea, it combines in its landscape the ruggedness of rocky outcrops and cliffs with the soft shapes of hills and mountains, skirted by coastal lowlands. For those who stay only briefly the scenery is what the Dingle experience is all about: the view of the Blasket Islands from Slea Head; the harbours, mountains, cliffs and strands; the view from the Connor Pass. Indeed, every part of the peninsula offers attractive and often dramatic views.

Roads lead over the mountains and along the coasts between irregular grids of mortarless stone walls surrounding small fields. The main road from Tralee divides at Camp: one route continues along the northern coast to Castlegregory, dividing again when one road turns towards Cloghane and another rises high to the Connor Pass over the mountains to Dingle. The other route from Camp rises to a mountain pass above *Gleann na nGealt*, the beautiful "valley of the mad", and descends to Anascaul and thence, after a series of hairpin bends, to Lispole and a long straight road to Dingle. From the direction of Killarney and Castlemaine another road enters the peninsula along a narrow coastal strip beneath the Slieve Mish mountains past the beautiful long strand at Inch and turns inland through a pass to Anascaul.

The Connor Pass road is undoubtedly the most dramatic route to take, though it is not suitable for heavy vehicles or caravans. As it swings

towards the south it rises at the side of a large valley formed by glaciers that came from a semi-circle of coums or corries in the surrounding mountains. From the top of the pass there are breathtaking views in fine weather of lowlands, mountains and sea.

High vantage points provide the best position from which to take in the sweep of the landscape, and most of the main roads on the peninsula cross mountains at passes. The road to Dingle via Anascaul does not rise as high as the Connor Pass, but it is high enough to provide magnificent views of the coast of Tralee and Brandon Bays, of the landscape on the southern side of the mountain range, and of the Iveragh Peninsula across Dingle Bay.

To the west of Dingle the most scenic route winds around the coast via Ventry to Slea Head, from which the view of the Blasket Islands is a sight that stops many visitors in their tracks. From Slea Head the road continues along the coast to Dunquin, thence to Ballyferriter, from which one road crosses by *Mám na Goaithe*, the windy pass, to Ventry; another goes further north to the *mám* at *Baile na nÁth* (Ballynana), the townland of the height. From this pass one road drops down to Milltown and Dingle while another continues north to Kilmalkedar, Ballydavid and Feohanagh, and meets a road which leads along the foot of Mount Brandon to a low pass back to Dingle.

From Dingle the Connor Pass road rises steeply, and in its higher reaches rocky mountain slopes and cliffs – at one point named *Faill na Seamróg*, the shamrock cliff – tower above to the left. At the bottom of the descent from Connor Pass to the north the road swings right to Castlegregory and Camp, and turns left to Cloghane and Brandon, finally coming to a halt on the cliffs at Brandon Point. From here there is a fine view of Brandon and Tralee Bays, the spit of sand out to the Maharees, and the whole northern side of the peninsula, while above and behind stands the imposing mass of Mount Brandon.

These are the main routes through the peninsula, each of them opening up a landscape rich in visual variety and interest. But there are also countless roads off the main routes and countless narrow bohareens, or country lanes, and for visitors who have time to do more than drive once through the peninsula, getting off the beaten track is the best way to explore the area.

The hills, coastline and countryside yield their qualities most readily to the walker. There is a depth in the appeal of the landscape which goes beyond the contemplation of beautiful scenery, for the countryside is dotted with the historical remains and artefacts of past centuries. The Dingle Peninsula possesses a quite extraordinary concentration of archaeological sites. These are not massive structures of great splendour, such as Newgrange or Stonehenge; but they are in their modesty more characteristic of the ages from which they survive. In the number that have survived in this small area lies a magnificence and splendour of its own.

The archaeological remains testify physically to the rich culture of the past, and the peninsula is also an exceptionally rich repository of folk-lore and of Irish traditional culture. Largely isolated in recent centuries from the mainstream of European and Irish economic, social and cultural change, Dingle, in common with other parts of the west of Ireland, long maintained traditional values and customs. Today in the area to the west of Dingle town Irish is very much the first language; many of the ancient customs which were observed for many centuries and had their origins before the advent of Christianity have died out in the last sixty years, but some survive. Some holy wells are still visited for annual devotions, and the day after Christmas Day is celebrated with the festival of "hunting the wren". Traditional music and dance play an important part in many people's lives, despite the counter-attractions of multinational pop culture, and the traditional small boats of ancient design, the *naomhóga* or curraghs, are still built and used.

For many people the most abiding impression, and one which has drawn visitors back year after year, is perhaps the most difficult to define. It has to do with the pace and rhythm of life, about which there is a subtle joke to the effect that the Irish language lacks a word that conveys the same sense of urgency as the Spanish *mañana*. It has to do with lifestyle, with a certain sense of ease, calm and relaxation. There is no one word that adequately describes it, but it is expressed in chance encounters. Visitors stop to ask for directions and find themselves drawn into conversations which are long, fascinating and charming. People used to the coldness of New York, Frankfurt or London are surprised to find the person next to them at the counter of a Dingle pub commenting upon the weather and wondering if they are enjoying their visit, where they have come from, how long they are staying and what they think of the present state of the world. However, a great deal of change occurred during the 1990s. Tourist numbers and facilities increased and prosperity grew substantially, and those involved in tourism increasingly spoke in terms of Dingle as a product to be promoted, adopting the full panoply of modern marketing perspectives. Partly the change was generational, with more young people happily able to remain living in the area. Nevertheless, there remains a certain laid-back informality, which visitors who stay for a while soon find is part of the experience, part of the attraction of the place.

Inevitably, the visitor's response to Dingle is an individual one. Many visit for the contact with Irish spoken in a natural, native way and for the insight that offers them into Irish life and culture. Others visit because it can be a kind of paradise for the hill walker; others to observe sea-birds or the arctic alpine flora. For many the atmosphere of simply being there, of impromptu meetings or musical sessions in pubs, is like a restoring breath of fresh air to which they will wish constantly to return. There must be few for whom the surrounding presence of the sea does not provide abiding images: the fishing boats in Dingle Harbour, the long sweeps of strand on the northern coastline, at Inch, Ventry and Smerwick; the sound between the Blasket Islands and Dunmore Head; the black *naomhóga* at Dunquin Harbour; the power of sea against rocks at Clogher and Brandon Creek.

The peninsula's position at the extreme western edge of Europe gives it a dramatic setting as it faces into the vastness of the Atlantic. It has also meant that its history has been shaped both by isolation from the more developed countries of Europe and by periods of close trading contact with Europe. What attracts many visitors to the area has much to do with the comparative isolation – from intensive economic development, from the central political, social and cultural concerns of the industrialised nations. Elements of the ancient cultural well-spring of Indo-European civilisation survived here long after they had been obliterated elsewhere; in terms of physical remains, the lack of economic development and the prevalence of superstitious inhibitions have meant that a great number of archaeological sites are still intact.

More recently many of the elements that give the Dingle Peninsula its particular character have been under heavy attack from modernising influences. Physically an enormous change in the very scenery of the peninsula has been taking place, and continues, as spruce trees march in ever more massive battalions across the landscape, which used to be characterised by long, uninterrupted stretches of blanket bog. The comparative prosperity of recent decades has enabled people to build new homes, and many have opted for singly sited white bungalows, which are now scattered over the countryside, with particular concentrations in strip developments along the roadsides. The strongest influence on the area is no longer farming or fishing; rather, it is tourism, and there has been debate in recent years, with some believing that the more tourists and the more tourist developments of any kind the better, while others have questioned how much tourism and of what kind is appropriate. Modernisation and prosperity are very welcome in themselves, but they do bring changes which place both old virtues and old vices under threat, and different people view such changes differently. However, it is still true to say that the life of the area possesses distinctive characteristics; that there is an elaborative and imaginative quality to local speech – most marked in Irish but also present in English. But these are qualities which reveal themselves to visitors who stay for a while and who have an ear for such things.

In what follows the attempt is to convey, in moving through the peninsula, examples of the elements that are characteristic of the area. It is not possible to provide information about everything; nor would one wish to. After all, the best kind of exploration is the kind you do yourself. There are many archaeological remains on the peninsula: there are fine megalithic graves, standing stones and early Christian settlements, not to mention ringforts, ogham stones and castles. The archaeological survey of the Dingle Peninsula, published in 1986, proved a four-year task for a team of archaeologists. And so, in this book, I have given detailed background in relation to just one example of each kind of archaeological site, while others are mentioned more briefly. To be comprehensive about the archaeology, folklore and history of the area would require many books: quite apart from archaeology, some sixty books have come out of the Blasket Islands, Dunquin and Ballyferriter alone; and the archives in the Department of Folklore in University College Dublin include some 100,000 pages of material from the Dingle Peninsula.

There is a luxury of material and of choice. The choices taken in this book of where to stop on the road and look in some detail would certainly not be everyone's choices; there are things and places described which other observers would consider insignificant, just as there are places and things not described which perhaps should have been. But the area is genuinely rich in all kinds of interest, and if this book succeeds in providing some information about every part of the peninsula while leaving an appetite for more, then it will have succeeded in its purpose.

An Introduction to History and Prehistory

THIS BOOK DESCRIBES, amongst other things, many of the archaeological sites and some of the history of the Dingle Peninsula. For the sake of convenience both archaeology and history are commonly divided up into ages and periods. These divisions are artificial to an extent, the dates are approximate, and in reality the characteristics of each category overlapped to a considerable extent.

THE STONE AGES (UP TO 2000 BC)

1. Palaeolithic: Early Stone Age

Cave-dwellers inhabited Europe in the palaeolithic period from 50,000 BC to 9000 BC.

2. Mesolithic: Middle Stone Age

From 9000 BC in Europe, and 6000 BC in Ireland, hunting and food collecting people fished on coasts and in rivers and hunted at the edges of dense forests; some lived amongst sandhills on diets largely of shellfish. Shell middens of mesolithic type have been found on the Dingle Peninsula, but the way of life they represented probably continued well into the next age and perhaps beyond.

3. Neolithic: Late Stone Age

The Neolithic Age, characterised by the development of agriculture and increases in population, began in Ireland some time between 5000 BC and 4000 BC and yielded to the Metal Ages in about 2000 BC. This was the age of the megalith (or big stone), of standing stones and graves, though these were also characteristic of the Bronze Age. No defensive structures have been found, but field systems from this period are some-times exposed when blanket bog is removed; so a picture emerges of a people peacefully taming the edges of forests, cultivating the soil and domesticating animals, living for the most part in relatively upland areas where the forest was less dense.

THE METAL AGES (2000 BC TO 400 AD)

1. The Copper Age

The south-west of Ireland was, from neolithic times, on a major trade route between the Mediterranean and Scandinavia. The Beaker people, originally from North Africa, settled in Europe and in the south-west of Ireland, where they mined the rich copper deposits. Indeed, the earliest known copper mines in Europe, dated to between 2300 and 2100 BC, have recently been identified on Ross Island in Loch Laune, one of the

Killarney lakes. A substantial export trade in metal goods and a significant development of civilisation and prosperity became centred during this period in Kerry and west Cork.

2. The Bronze Age

Bronze – a mixture of copper and tin – began to be manufactured from 1800 BC and gold from 2000 BC. Strikingly beautiful work was done in both gold and bronze – collars of beaten gold, bracelets and fasteners, bronze halberds, daggers, swords and axes – and was exported to every part of Europe. Both earthen ringforts and stone cahers began to be built in this period, but these forms of construction were not to flourish until early Christian times. A type of archaeological site from the Bronze Age is the *fulacht fiadh*, the outdoor cooking place which features in the tales of Fionn Mac Cumhail.

3. The Iron Age

Dating from 800 BC to 400 AD, the Iron Age was marked by the arrival of the Celts, who had achieved dominance and prosperity in continental Europe. Little is known about this period in the south-west of Ireland, but the physical elements suggest that the Dingle Peninsula was a very important centre of Iron Age society. The characteristic surviving structure of this time – very much a characteristic of the Belgic Celts – was the promontory fort; the two highest and most impressive hilltop forts of this kind in Ireland are on the peninsula, and every natural coastal promontory is fortified.

THE EARLY CHRISTIAN PERIOD (400 AD TO 1200 AD)

This was probably the most notable time in the history of the peninsula, which became a focal point of early Christian activity. About sixty sites of early Christian settlements have been identified, most of them at the western end of the peninsula, and at Fahan there was a unique development of "beehive hut" (*clochán*) dwellings. It is believed that the Dingle Peninsula became the centre of a longstanding maritime pilgrimage which extended along the whole of the Atlantic coast of Ireland and beyond, to Scotland, Iceland, Greenland, and even North America.

The *Corca Dhuibhne* people, who lived also on the northern side of the Iveragh Peninsula, seem to have lived in peace, paying tribute to their Gaelic overlords in Cashel. Probably the originators of ogham writing, their most famous daughter was the early seventh century poetess Liadan, the story of whose love for Cuirithir is a classic which resembles *Tristan and Isolde*.

The artefacts of this period include the oratories, cross-slabs and *clocháin* within stone enclosure walls of the religious settlements. Vikings raided the coast in the ninth century but made less impact than in other parts of Ireland, though they seem to have settled at Smerwick, the large harbour in the west of the peninsula.

Both secular and religious life suffered a decline into social and political disorder in the tenth century, which continued into the eleventh and twelfth centuries. The focus of religious activity became the remarkable missionary movement in continental Europe, which established monasteries from Ratisbon to Kiev. In the course of a long reform of the Irish church, Kilmalkedar – where the church is twelfth century – seems to have retained an importance, as did the Mount Brandon pilgrimage.

THE ENGLISH INVASION (1200 AD TO THE PRESENT)

Anglo-Normans

The Anglo-Norman invasion ushered in three centuries of control by the Geraldines – the Fitzgeralds. Flemish, Welsh, English and Norman colonists settled, bringing names such as Hussey, Rice, Trant, Ferriter, Browne and Walsh, which were to remain prominent family names to the present day. This invasion also ushered in an era of closer control by the Pope of the Church in Ireland.

Conquest

The feudal order established by the Anglo-Normans came into conflict with the English administration in the sixteenth century, a conflict sharpened by the advent of bitter religious divisions with the English attempt to impose the reformation. A long, violent process of rebellion and conquest concluded with the nation utterly crushed by the end of the seventeenth century. The old Gaelic order was gone, the feudal lords were defeated; administration was in the hands of the Protestant ascendancy, acting in the interests of England.

Towards Nationhood
The English administration suppressed Irish Catholicism and culture and political, social and economic freedom. Rural agitation against tithes and enclosures was widespread in the eighteenth century, but some prosperity came to the Dingle Peninsula during the brief flowering of the linen industry. Famine devastated the country (1845–48) and was followed by emigration and evictions. The late nineteenth century saw the growth of a new Irish nationalist movement, and the Easter Rising of 1916 signalled the beginning of the end of British rule.

In the independent state established in twenty-six of Ireland's thirty-two counties, the west remained economically undeveloped and emigration continued. The 1970s were a prosperous decade in the Dingle Peninsula; many new houses were built and living standards improved significantly. A high rate of emigration of young people in the 1980s began to be reversed in the 1990s; there was a new influx of people coming to live in the area, and the number, range and quality of jobs available increased.

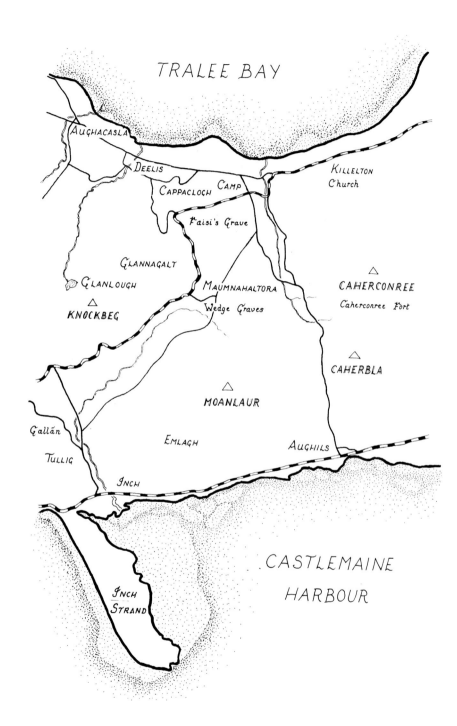

TRALEE BAY

Aughacasla

Deelis

Cappacloch Camp

Killelton
Church

Faisi's Grave

Glannagalt

Glanlough

△
CAHERCONREE

Caherconree Fort

△
KNOCKBEG

Maumnahaltora

Wedge Graves

△
CAHERBLA

△
MOANLAUR

Gallán

Emlagh

Aughils

Tullig

Inch

CASTLEMAINE

HARBOUR

Inch
Strand

From Derrymore to Inch

THERE ARE TWO roads into the peninsula: one in the north and one in the south, each on narrow strips of lowland between the sea and the Slieve Mish mountains. Rising above 2500 feet (762 metres) in parts, this mountain range was the scene of prehistoric battles, which were recorded in legend as having been part of the "Milesian invasion". The Milesians, meaning "soldiers of Spain", are said in the legends to have been Gaels who came originally from Egypt, settled in Spain, and invaded Ireland in 1700 BC. Their first battle took place here in the mountains where Banba, a queen of the *Tuatha Dé Danainn* – the people of Ireland at that time – opposed them. Magic was employed on both sides but gave way to fighting, in which Scota and Fás, queens of the Milesians, were amongst those killed. But the Milesians won not only the battle in Slieve Mish but the war for the conquest of Ireland. The three kings and queens of the *Tuatha Dé Danainn* were killed and their people were driven underground into forts and mounds where they became, in effect, the fairies.

As the visitor enters the peninsula from the town of Tralee, which has developed many interesting and varied tourist attractions in recent years, the bright expanse of Tralee Bay comes into full view at Derrymore (*An Doire Mhór*, the large oak wood), where the long strand is a favoured bathing place and caravans punctuate the coastline. In contrast to the largely rocky south and west coast of the peninsula, the northern coast from Derrymore to Cloghane offers mile after mile of sandy, safe beaches, which also provide excellent opportunities for angling.

The northern part of the peninsula, the area from Brandon Point to Derrymore, which is bounded by Mount Brandon and the mountain range that runs down the centre of the peninsula like a spine, is known as Letteragh, or *Leith-triúch*, which means "half a barony". Throughout the history of the area the mountains have constituted a considerable barrier and there have been great differences between Letteragh and the rest of the peninsula. In particular, Letteragh was settled before the advent of Christianity by one tribal group (the *Uí Fhearba,* part of the *Ciarraighe*), while the rest of the peninsula was settled by another people, whose name became the name of the peninsula in Irish: *Corca Dhuibhne.*

In Derrymore itself there are seven ringforts in varying states of preservation, the most notable of which, in Derrymore East, has double banks and fosses. It has an extensive souterrain with several chambers, and there are ruins of stone huts, but it is very much overgrown with briars, gorse and trees.

A small distance above the road in Derrymore runs the route of the Dingle Way, and near this wonderful walking route is a place where spiders' nests can be found, those miraculous constructions which exist only where there is no disturbance from the feet or hooves of humans or animals.

About a mile from Derrymore on the road towards Camp, a laneway leads up to the left at a driveway to several large, new houses. To the right off this driveway is a narrow track, part of the Dingle Way, which leads to a stream. Beyond the stream lies the abandoned, ruined village of Killelton (*Cill Eilthín*, St Eltan's church), where ivy grows profusely on the cluster of buildings, its thick roots clinging to the rough surfaces of the stone walls. Tall nettles bar doorways; holly, fuchsia, ferns, brambles, thistles, honeysuckle and foxgloves abound; butterflies and crickets enjoy the profusion. The hill behind the ruined houses is densely covered with holly; and hawks may sometimes be seen here against the backdrop of the mountains of Caherconree and Baurtregaum.

Once this quiet and deserted place with its magnificent view over Tralee Bay was a community of many families, but they were evicted by the landlord in the nineteenth century. Later, three brothers lived here, farming the land around collectively without benefit of fences. But the historical interest of Killelton extends much further back.

On the left at the west of the village lie the ruins of an early oratory. The interior of the oratory measures 5 metres long and about 3.5 metres wide. A particular and evident feature is the plinth at the bottom of the north and south walls, a feature characteristic of a number of early oratories. During restoration in 1984 a holed stone similar to pivot stones at Gallarus oratory was found, and this ruined shell of a building must once have been similar both to the oratories at Reask and Raingiléis, now also ruined, and to Gallarus, which is wonderfully well preserved. The restoration has certainly changed the appearance of the site from its overgrown state of a few years ago, and the height of the walls of the oratory has been substantially increased in the process. The oratory is surrounded by low walls which make an almost square enclosure, within which there are also the scant remains of two rectangular buildings.

The first account of this site appeared in the *Ulster Archaeological Journal* in 1860, and the author of the report noted the local belief that beneath it lay the grave of a Milesian princess, called Fás, or Faisi. In 1898 Mary Hickson reported in the *Journal of the Royal Society of Antiquaries of Ireland* in much greater detail. Not only was this the grave of Fás, she maintained, but also the area from Killelton to Maumnahaltora – some four miles south-west – had been known for "between 20 to 30 centuries" as Glenfás. However, both the Ordnance Survey and local historian

Doncha Ó Conchúir place the grave of Fás two miles away on the west bank of the Finglas River.

The road between Killelton and Camp bends sharply at the Curraduff bridge, and just above the road bridge stands the old Tralee and Dingle Railway viaduct. As David G. Rowlands writes in *The Tralee & Dingle Railway* (Bradford Barton, 1977), this line had "some of the most frightful curves and gradients ever engineered on a light railway". On Whit Monday of 1893, Locomotive Number One came off the rails and fell thirty feet to the river; three men and ninety pigs were killed. To ease the bend here, another bridge was built in 1907 a few hundred yards upstream.

Opened in 1891, the 3-foot gauge railway, with a branch line to Castlegregory, was extraordinarily slow and accident-prone. Undulating between sea level and 680 feet (207 metres) above, trains were often stopped and sand spread on the tracks to give sufficient grip to tackle gradients. In 1939 the Castlegregory branch was closed, in 1944 the Tralee-Dingle goods service ended, largely because of the wartime coal shortage; and from 1947 until closure in 1953 the only business was the cattle train for Dingle Fair on the last Saturday of each month. Less than a mile along the road to the east from the viaduct bridge, the water tower at Knockglassmore is all that remains of Castlegregory Junction; on the opposite side of the road Fitzgerald's, or the "Junction Bar", was much frequented by railwaymen and passengers alike and was the cause of many delays.

In Knockglassmore where the Finglas River enters the sea is the easternmost coastal promontory fort on the Dingle Peninsula. One of the principal types of archaeological site characteristic of the area, the coastal promontory fort encloses a triangle of land, combining natural cliff defences with made defences such as banks, ditches and walls. Here cliffs fall away to the north and south of this overgrown fort, while the eastern side is defended by an earthen bank and, possibly, a fosse.

In the field to the west of the Curraduff bridge there once stood an Anglo-Norman castle of the same basic design as several others on the peninsula, but nothing remains of it now.

From the bend beside the bridge a road signposted "Scenic Route" leads south into the valley of the Finglas River and through wild hillside country to the southern shore of the peninsula at Aughils. Known as *Bóthar na gCloch*, the rocky road, it leads through some impressive scenery where the Slieve Mish mountains tower steeply above to the east, Tralee Bay lies to the north, and Castlemaine Harbour, the Kerry mainland and the Iveragh Peninsula are spread out to the south. Even on a cloudy day, or when the evening air is thick, the countryside here has a unique and lonely splendour. Around Coumastabla are woodcocks, and on the higher reaches of the road are snipe and sometimes grouse and wheatears, which are found in similar upland areas throughout the peninsula.

There are many hares on the hillside and the walker may easily be startled as one appears suddenly very close at hand. Seen against the skyline a little higher up a slope, or in mist, which makes all animals and birds seem larger, hares can often appear extraordinarily big. Which perhaps goes a little way towards explaining a strange story told on the southern side of the hill, which features a hare so large it wears the saddle of a horse.

The promontory fort of Caherconree in the townland of Beheenagh occupies a commanding position, at a height of 2050 feet (625 metres), above *Bóthar na gCloch* and the Finglas Valley. It stands at a physical frontier, where the Slieve Mish range ends, a frontier between the peninsula and the mainland, between east and west; it stands also on the boundary between the baronies of *Corca Dhuibhne* and *Truich an Aicme* and it marked an ancient tribal boundary. A large projecting spur of the mountain, visible from many miles away to the west, is cut across on its north-eastern side by a wall 350 feet (110 metres) long, forming a triangular enclosure protected on its north-western and south-western sides by steep cliffs. The area enclosed is about two acres. The dry-stone wall stands to a maximum height of nearly 3 metres. It is massively thick and in sections of it the inner face features three distinct steps.

This was the fortress of Cú Raoi Mac Daire and it features in the "Red Branch" sagas of the Ulster heroes. A respected tribal chief and demigod, perhaps even the sun-god of the Belgae, Cú Raoi possessed many magical powers: he could adopt many forms, often terrifying to his enemies, and even when absent he could defend the fort at night by setting it spinning. In one story, the three champions of Ulster – the legendary Cúchulainn, Conall and Laegaire – resorted to him to resolve their dispute as to which of them was worthiest. They were instructed to take turns in guarding Caherconree, and there Cú Raoi attacked each of them in the form of demons. Conall and Laegaire were pitched over the wall by the monsters, but Cúchulainn stood his ground. However, he thought that the other two had jumped the wall as proof of their prowess, and decided to emulate them; he succeeded in an epic leap, but only just. On a later occasion a disguised Cú Raoi again intervened in events that established the superiority of Cúchulainn.

Relations between Cúchulainn and Cú Raoi became soured after a raid on the Isle of Man. When Cúchulainn and his comrades had laid siege to the Manx chief's fort, but found no way to take it, a disguised Cú Raoi struck a bargain that he would help them in return for the pick of the spoils. Having taken the fort, they came to the division of the booty and Cú Raoi picked the chief's daughter, Blathnaid; but Cúchulainn wanted her, too, and would not accept his choice. Cú Raoi's decisive response was to take the lot, including Blathnaid, and head for home. Cúchulainn overtook and challenged him near Cashel but was defeated and left by Cú Raoi buried up to his armpits with his head shaved and covered with cowdung.

Desire for Blathnaid was augmented by the fiercer desire to avenge his disgrace: a year later, when his hair had grown to a respectable length, Cúchulainn set out on Cú Raoi's trail. Guided by mythical birds, he

arrived in the valley of Caherconree, where he met Blathnaid. Together they plotted Cú Raoi's death. Cúchulainn and his army assembled near Camp on November 1st and soon the river ran white with milk – the sign from Blathnaid that all was prepared for his attack. She had insisted that the smallness of the stones in the wall of the fort detracted from its prestige, and Cú Raoi had sent his men to get large stones; the fort thus unguarded, she gave the sign to Cúchulainn.

As the attackers worked their way up the mountainside, Blathnaid combed Cú Raoi's hair in the gateway; she brought him inside, then bathed him and, taking his sword, put him to bed. Cúchulainn and his men stormed into the fort: Cú Raoi fought hard with hands and feet, but he and his son were killed and the buildings in the fort burned. Cúchulainn returned to Ulster with Blathnaid, also taking Cú Raoi's druid, Feircheirtne. Later this druid exacted tragic revenge for Cú Raoi by grabbing Blathnaid and leaping off a cliff with her in his arms.

Where a stream crosses *Bóthar na gCloch* at Beheenagh, posts painted white and red have been erected on the right-hand side of the glen, indicating a route to the fort. Another, rather less safe route is to climb up the ridge at the left of the glen; it is steeper, but gives a fine view of the "gate" – a gap in the projecting rocks of the spur that looks for all the world like a made gateway. On the spur below the rock "gateway" at the apex of the triangular promontory are large, deep gashes and holes in the hillside. These are the consequences of a major geological "fault", or rupture, called the Caherconree Fault, which may be traced from here to Minard Head, 15 miles away. Some of these holes possess unusually rich growths of mosses and ferns. Walkers who encounter mist, which descends very rapidly, should exercise extreme caution. Further up the mountain is a stone called Fionn MacCumhail's Chair.

The view on a clear day from Caherconree is magnificent: to the west are the Blasket Islands, Mount Brandon and the Dingle Peninsula; to the south MacGillycuddy's Reeks, and to the north Loop Head.

After making the detour on *Bóthar na gCloch*, especially if one has climbed to the fort, refreshments of one kind and another may be next on the agenda, and the village of Camp can cater well. Either take the same route back to the bend at Curraduff Bridge and turn left to Camp, or take the parallel road that branches off to the left after Coumastabla

Woods, crosses the river and leads directly into Camp. This second route crosses the old Tralee-Dingle road, a surfaced and very straight section of which leads uphill to the left; across the river a green track rises equally straight towards Killelton. In both directions this old route has been taken into the Dingle Way.

Continuing from the junction with the old road towards Camp, in a field on the right just before a cluster of buildings above the metal railway bridge lies the reputed grave of Fás, one of the Milesian queens. A fallen *gallán,* or megalithic standing stone, is marked with ogham, the early form of writing made by cutting groups of lines, an inscription in half-uncial script, and a simple incised cross. The ogham reads: conunett MOQI CON(U)R(I); the half-uncials read: FECT CUNURI.

Camp is where Cúchulainn waited for the sign from Blathnaid, but nowadays it is a popular centre for visitors with more peaceful intentions. Horse-drawn caravans stop here, and there are shops, a church, a post office (on the lower, Castlegregory road) and four fine pubs, two in the upper village, two in the lower.

The main road to Anascaul and Dingle continues west from Camp, opening up views of the countryside, coast and mountains. It swings sharply left and south above the legendary "valley of the mad", *Gleann na nGealt.* The railway used to pursue its precipitous route on the right hand side of the road here and some of its bridges can still be seen; it comes as little surprise to learn that a train was blown off the tracks by a gust of wind on this stretch.

Very shortly after reaching the highest point on the road, another road leads off to the left at Maumnahaltora. There is a cluster of buildings just above the road and immediately before these are the stones of megalithic graves. Below the road is another one, well preserved, and the remains of several others. These megalithic tombs are some of the earliest stone structures in the region. They are neolithic, or Late Stone Age, in type, though they continued to be built into the Early Bronze Age. In these burials the bodies were burned, surrounded by walls of upright stones (orthostats) and roofed over by very large flat stones. The whole tomb was then usually covered with a pile of small stones and clay, making a cairn; in general these mounds no longer remain on the graves. A particular feature of the megalithic tombs in this area is their wedge

shape: one end is wider than the other, the head is higher than the foot, and they face west. The finding of contemporary field fences at similar excavated sites suggests that such tombs were built within the settlements of the people who erected them.

A well near the graves, which has long been dry and covered by growth, was reputed to have contained a sacred fish, a pre-Christian conception which occurs also at *Tobar Naomh Molaige* at Ballywiheen in the west of the peninsula. In Christian times the well here came to be dedicated to Saints Peter, Paul and John, between whose feasts pilgrimages were made annually, a practice which continued even after the well had dried up and only ended within the last thirty or forty years. The name of the place – *Mám na hAltóra*, pass of the altar – probably derives simply from the shape of the horizontal slabs of stone on the tombs. One of the stones above the road is decorated with cup-and-circle marks and lines, in a style of decoration described as rock art. In recent years the landowner has been unwilling to allow access to these graves, so the visitor should just look at them from the road.

A large bog at Slieve extends to the south of Maumnahaltora between the Emlagh River and the hills of Knockbrack, Moanlaur and Knockmore. Silent and empty for most of the year, turf cutting starts in May and, up to the recent past, many local people from miles around could be seen working the plots for which they have the rights of turbary,

as it is called – in other words to extract the turf for fuel. It is hard work, usually carried out by whole families. Large quantities are needed, for turf yields less than half the heat of coal; and the wetness of the bog means that the turves are about eight times heavier when cut than when they have dried and are ready to be burned.

First the top is removed to a depth of a foot, and then the cutting can begin. The special tool used, a *sleán*, has a narrow steel blade with a right-angled wing and a straight, narrow shaft. The size of the blade varies according to the size of turf to be cut: in a very wet bog the turves are cut larger to allow for the greater shrinkage when dried. After lying on the ground for one or two weeks the turves are "footed"; that is, they are set in small stacks to catch the wind. During succeeding weeks they are turned and gradually built into larger stacks until they are dry and ready to be taken to the house, where they are placed against the gable or in a shed.

Turf, or peat, came into its own as fuel in the sixteenth and seventeenth centuries after extensive forest clearance, though its use goes back many more centuries, especially in areas where there were few trees available for fuel. It played a vital role in the subsistence economy, for although there was little to eat for the rural population, at least they could keep warm with the freely available and abundant turf. Resinous "splits" of fir from the bogs also provided lights for the home, and larger pieces of preserved wood were used as timber in building. The preservative qualities of the bog were also exploited for storage, and many finds have been made of "bog butter", not only in Ireland but also in Iceland, India, Morocco and Scandinavia. For the archaeologist the lower layers of bogs can be especially productive, yielding ancient weapons and tools, megalithic tombs, field fences, cultivation marks and signs of changes in vegetation and climate. Lowland blanket bog such as this is a rare ecotype of considerable interest.

In a part of this bog where trees now grow the body of a child of the seventeenth or eighteenth century was found in 1950. With red-brown hair, it wore a dress like a pinafore and possibly a cloak and other garments. Aged between about six and eight, it was probably male, and with it were a double-sided wooden comb and a leather purse containing flax fibres and a ball of woollen thread.

The route of the Dingle Way passes through the bog and on through the forest towards Inch. The main road continues beside and above the bog through the wooded Slieve and on to Lougher, just after which is a crossroads. Anyone with a particular interest in sighting lines between megalithic standing stones might like to do a little exploring from this crossroads. Much has been written about "ley lines" and alignments, perhaps the best known study of which remains *The Old Straight Track* by Alfred Watkins. Familiarity with relevant sites and the topography of the area does not lead me to support any elaborate theories about alignments, but it is certainly the case that most of the standing stones were placed in highly visible positions. Beyond that, they often stand in interesting relationships to each other and to the landscape, and it can be fascinating to speculate about what might have been the intentions of the first farmers who erected them and what might have been their full significance for that early society.

About half a mile uphill from the crossroads, in a field to the left of the road, is a fallen *gallán*. If one stands on the field fence beside it and looks south-south-east towards the gap in the hills, another *gallán* is visible sticking up like a needle in the middle of the gap on a hillock at Tullig, almost two miles away. From this fallen stone, too, at least one other *gallán* is visible to the west, and it is easy to gain the impression that these standing stones are pointing out a route or directions of some kind.

Several boulders inscribed with rock art were found in Lougher, and one of them has been taken into the Heritage Centre in Ballyferriter, where it can easily be studied. It features a large cup-and-three-circles with a radial line running from the cup; there are also about six other circles on it, and an incomplete cup-and-circle.

Back at the crossroads the road to the left off the main road leads past the road from the forestry at Emlagh, past the *gallán* at Tullig, and down to Inch. A right turn here along the road from Castlemaine brings one to Inch Strand.

Megalithic remains, such as those at Maumnahaltora, are the earliest stone structures; but at Inch remains of earlier, mesolithic or Middle Stone Age type lie in the sandhills. Just as the wedge graves, although neolithic in type, continued to be built into the Early Bronze Age, so, too, characteristically mesolithic sites may have been created by much later peoples. A mile along the long spit of sand are the Maghaglass sandhills, within which stands a midden – a large pile of shells – on a high raised beach; to the east is the Gubranna midden, measuring some 600 yards by 60 yards. The ancient shore dwellers of Inch gathered and ate shellfish and lived amongst their piles of empty shells. Thin seams of charcoal may be seen at parts of the middens exposed by erosion where fires were made, and hammer stones, grain rubbers, bones, axes and other evidence of these primitive people have been found.

Further investigation may reveal a date for the earliest occupation of the Inch middens, but it is likely that they resulted from a stage of society in which the new farming mode of life was combined with the older way of food-gathering and hunting at the edges of the forests, beside streams and at the coasts. Later accretions certainly exist in the middens: the shellfish remained a readily available source of food. In an account of a military expedition to inspect the fort of *Dún an Óir* at Smerwick in 1580, an officer noted in his diary that the company took advantage of the abundance of cockles while camping overnight at Inch. As recently as the turn of the century cockles were being taken from here, boiled on the spot, and sold – their shells being left to add to the middens. During the Famine, too, starving people reverted to the food source of their early ancestors.

The position of the strand, jutting out into Dingle Bay across the mouth of Castlemaine Harbour, made it a favoured location for the activities of "wreckers" in the eighteenth century. During gales a lantern was fixed to a horse's head, and as it grazed the bobbing movement of the light could easily be mistaken for that of a ship. Thinking they had safe passage, ships would plough straight into the spit of sand, and the wreckers reaped their cargoes. A story is told, too, that the first tea on the peninsula came from a wreck on Inch Strand. Not knowing what it was, a group of people boiled it for two hours, let it cool, and then ate the leaves!

Nowadays Inch is above all a wonderful place for swimming: its long, golden strand provides acres of space for beach football, frisbee-throwing, sand castles, or simply lying in the sun, and it is a place to which gliding enthusiasts come. It is not sheltered from wind, which can make it chilly at times, but on a gentle, sunny day it can be the best beach in the world. Facing west, it is a place to see the sun set as the breakers roll in along Dingle Bay. Small wonder that it provided a location for two films – *The Playboy of the Western World* (1962) and

Ryan's Daughter (1969). In recent years it has also attracted great numbers of anglers, mostly from England, in search of bass.

In the surroundings of Castlemaine Harbour, between Inch and Glenbeigh, an unusual Lusitanian amphibian is to be found, though with some difficulty as it stays beneath the sand during the day and emerges only at night. This is the natterjack toad, a prominent-eyed, warty, golden or olive creature; it occurs in south-west Scotland, England and the Mediterranean, but in Ireland only in Kerry. Also found in Castlemaine Harbour, but only in the winter, are brent geese, for which this area and Tralee Bay are their major wintering places in Ireland. The red-throated diver is a rare winter visitor to Inch, but the great northern diver is frequently seen here, as is the nightjar, which breeds at Inch and in other parts of the eastern end of the peninsula. While the eastern side of the Inch spit holds thousands of wildfowl and waders, the surf on the western side is the best place to see scoters in winter.

From Inch the road west along the coastal cliffs provides an excellent view out over Dingle Bay and to the Iveragh Peninsula. It swings right then, inland to Anascaul; to visit the village of Anascaul one should bear right and then turn right.

INCH BEACH COTTAGES

Inch Beach Cottages comprise a cluster of 8 luxury four star self-catering cottages, located just 200 yards from Inch Beach (made famous by *Ryan's Daughter* and *The Playboy of the Western World*). Inch Beach Cottages have one of the finest and most beautiful locations in the world, overlooking Inch Beach and Dingle Bay and nestling between the Slieve Mish mountains to the north, and the MacGillycuddy Reeks to the south.

Tel: +353 66 9158118 & 9158333   Fax: 353 66 9158388
email: inch@iol.ie

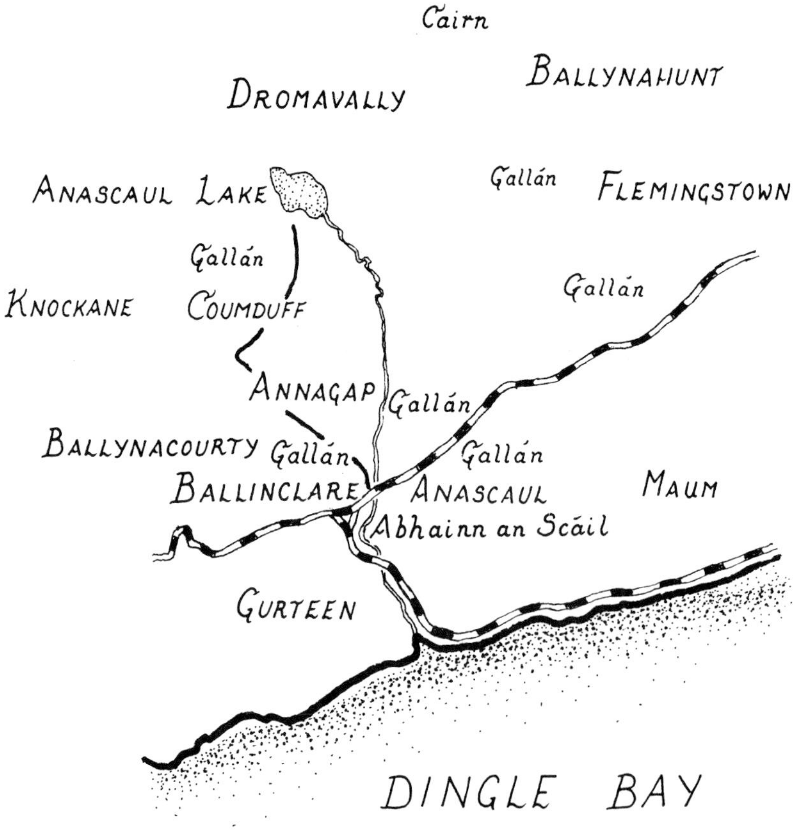

Cairn

BALLYNAHUNT

DROMAVALLY

Gallán   FLEMINGSTOWN

ANASCAUL LAKE

Gallán

Gallán

KNOCKANE   Gallán
COUMDUFF

ANNAGAP   Gallán

BALLYNACOURTY Gallán   Gallán

BALLINCLARE   ANASCAUL   MAUM
Abhainn an Scáil

GURTEEN

DINGLE BAY

ANASCAUL

ANASCAUL, NEAR THE junction of the Castlemaine and Tralee roads, is a village which has in recent years improved considerably in appearance. Derelict and other houses have been restored and renovated, and a welcome emphasis has been placed on the appropriate use and retention of local stone. There are new restaurants and guesthouses, renovated bars and a pottery, and the place presents a more colourful and pleasant face to the world than it did only a few years ago. In years gone by, Anascaul's fairs were for many centuries a vital focus for people from all over the peninsula. The Anglo-Normans, who established commercial fairs all over Ireland, settled here in the surrounding countryside in significant numbers, and their names are recorded in nearby townlands such as Ballynahunt and Flemingstown.

Well into the 1930s the fairs remained lively and crowded affairs. The entertainments were not mere frills on a mainly commercial occasion but, in true Gaelic spirit, were essential to the proceedings. The wheel of fortune, stalls selling humbugs, women in their best dresses and hats, men whose clothes echoed time spent in foreign parts, the three-card trickster, ballad singers, fiddlers, match-makers, peddlars and beggars – all combined to make a colourful social gathering as well as an occasion for business; and in the pubs the stories were told and news exchanged. This was true of a number of fairs on the peninsula but they were already in the 1930s being taken over by economic and social change; they became concentrated in fewer places and the dealing in livestock was removed to special marts.

Although the days of the fairs are gone Anascaul still boasts a large number of pubs for its small population. The most flamboyantly painted of all the pubs belonged to an equally flamboyant person, Dan Foley, and has found its way on to more than one popular postcard. Dan himself was a magician and a farmer as well as a publican, and his knowledge of local history could fill many more pages than this entire book. Another pub, the South Pole Inn, commemorates in its name its previous owner, Tom Crean, who was a noted polar explorer with Scott and Shackleton. Another famous son of Anascaul was Jerome Connor, sculptor of the *Lusitania* memorial at Cobh and the Robert Emmet statue, the original of which is in Washington and a copy of which stands in St Stephen's Green in Dublin. Building upon this heritage, energetic local community effort has achieved the foundation of a school of stone carving, which was opened at the end of 1999, and it is planned to create beside this school, at the confluence of three rivers, a Jerome Connor exhibition centre, which would exhibit not only work by the sculptor but also touring exhibitions, and a sculpture park and sculpture garden. The prosperity of the last decade, and in particular the boom in construction, has seen far more people able to remain in the Anascaul area, and their presence is reflected in a new social vitality. In addition to the time-honoured Ballinclare Fair, Anascaul now plays host to an annual magic weekend, an art and sculpture festival, and a walking festival.

From the Famine to the present day, as in other parts of Ireland, few have remained in Anascaul to work the land; many have emigrated and worked in Dublin, Britain, the United States and other parts of the world, returning occasionally to their homes; and for some time there was a tradition of the sons of Anascaul serving in the British navy.

The historical features of the Anascaul area divide roughly between the lowlands and the hills, and many factors both link and separate them. The earliest inhabitants lived mostly in the uplands, before the blanket bog formed. Later came one of the classic divisions of rural society – that between *baile* and *buaile*. *Baile* (the "Bally" of anglicised placenames) is the townland where the home lies; *buaile* is the upland milking place where the tenders of livestock often lived in small huts in the summer months. These lowland people went to the hill to tend sheep, goats and cattle, to hunt and to cut turf. The semi-nomadic movement to summer

pastures provided a refuge from authority and a link with the upland past, and contributed to the continuity of oral tradition.

Legends derived from the prehistoric past cling to the crags, ridges, peaks and lakes of the uplands. Folklore – the customs, beliefs and stories that informed and enriched the lives of the people – is, naturally enough, associated more with the lowlands, where it was elaborated amongst the clusters of dwellings. Most of the best known legends were written down from about the ninth century onwards; but there were also legends, sagas and stories which continued solely in oral tradition. One such is the story of the Giant, Cúchulainn and Scál ní Mhurnáin at Lough Anascaul.

Scál, a woman who lived near the lake, was attacked by a giant and appealed to Cúchulainn for help. At first he and the giant exchanged insults in verse across the lake, Cúchulainn standing on the top of Dromavally – the mountain to the east – and the giant standing on Knockmulanane to the west. Insults gave way to boulders and the battle raged for a week. The giant seems to have had a slight advantage since Knockmulanane is a little higher than Dromavally, and eventually he scored a direct hit, severely wounding Cúchulainn who let out a roar of pain. Hearing this, Scál believed her champion had been killed: she jumped in the lake and was drowned.

This simple story is believed to be of an early origin, perhaps descended from a myth of rivalry between two gods for the possession of a goddess. It resembles a common legend-type, in which a godly battle for the crops, for fertility and abundance, involves the confining of a female fiend, often in the form of a serpent, within a narrow place or a lake. It has been suggested that the female figure may represent famine or the earth-mother, but it also possible that what is reflected in the legend is a battle between women, who discovered agriculture, and men, who appropriated it.

Clearly his fight with the giant was not one of Cúchulainn's most successful encounters. Nevertheless, it is commemorated by two cairns on Dromavally. The most westerly of these, Cúchulainn's House, stands about 16 feet (5 metres) high and is about 75 feet (23 metres) in diameter. Its original diameter was about 50 feet (15 metres), but the stones of the cairn have spread beyond the retaining wall, traces of which can be seen. There is a large depression at the centre of the cairn, which may well be the result of burial chambers underneath having collapsed. Extending from the cairn is a line of about sixteen stones, some of which have fallen, and these measure between 6 feet 6 inches (2 metres) and just 1 foot 4 inches (.4 metre). From various points in the lowlands between Dromavally Bog and Ballynahunt, the points of the larger standing stones in this considerable alignment can be seen projecting from the ridge. About a mile (1.5 kilometres) away, at the eastern end of this mountain ridge, the cairn at Ballynahunt stands about 6 feet 6 inches (2 metres) high and is about 40 feet (12 metres) in diameter, and there is a retaining wall about 4 feet (1.2 metres) high around the western half of the perimeter of the cairn. Around the base are several sheepfolds built with stones from the cairn. The nearby trigonometrical station was also probably built with stones from the cairn.

Cairns can vary greatly in age, having continued to be built from the early prehistoric period to the present day. Most, but not all, cover burials of one kind or another, but some may simply commemorate an event or a person, or may mark an important boundary. Some are associated with Christian pilgrimages, where the stations were marked by cairns to which pilgrims constantly added stones.

Anascaul lake is a place of atmosphere and moods: resting in the bowl of the mountains, it is susceptible to sudden changes of light. A strange feature that may be noticed when the water level is particularly low is

what looks like an underwater building, with stones resembling chimneys projecting above the water. A building of a very different kind – a camouflaged lean-to – was built under the cliffs at the west of the lake by IRA men, nine of whom hid out there during the War of Independence. After the Lispole ambush one of the wounded was brought up here and later across the mountains on the old green track; and near by a cave held an arms cache.

From the lake a track continues into the glen and climbs its steep wall to the top of the mountain ridge. Here, under blanket bog beside the track, a Bronze Age halberd – a combination of a spear and battle-axe mounted on a long handle – was found. Two miles to the north-east lie the twin peaks of Beenoskee and Stradbally Mountain; but the track continues to the summer cattle pasture of Maghanaboe, to the north-west. Beside a stream above the ruins of houses the last wolf on the peninsula is said to have been killed, and the ledge is known as the Wolf's Step. Where a stream falls directly from nearly 500 feet the eroded basin is called the Devil's Hole.

Maghanaboe long provided the best way to cross the mountain ridge. The finding of the halberd beside the green track suggests its very early use, and there are indications that tracks also went from Maghanaboe into the high valley of Coumanare.

The old green track offers an excellent route for the present-day walker from the lake, across the ridge and down the length of the Glennahoo River valley to Ballyduff. From the middle of the ridge, where the line of the route becomes unclear, an easy approach to Beenoskee and Stradbally Mountain can be made. A great variety of views may be enjoyed on a clear day by ascending Knockmulanane near the Carrigblaher Cliffs, descending north-west to the boggy peneplain and turning right to the top of the saddle where the green track crosses. From here the cliffs above Glanteenassig, the glens of the waterfall, lie a little more than one-and-a-half miles (2.4 kilometres) east-south-east. After initially impressing with their silent emptiness the uplands can become monotonous to the eye; but the dullness of blanket bog is amply compensated for by the view from above Glanteenassig of the wooded valley and Tralee Bay beyond. *Gallâin* stand at the foot of Dromavally hill, and the southernslope was once the scene of berry-picking on the last Sunday in July. This tradition, which has been dead for many years now, occurred in many places as the last vestige of the ancient Celtic festival of Lughnasa, for the first fruits of the hillside were like a promise of fertility and a response to the people's offering of the first sheaf of corn to the god of the mountain.

The earliest inhabitants of the peninsula left their marks with the standing stones that seem to radiate from Lough Anascaul, but the most abundant evidence is of the early settled farmers, whose ringfort style of building spans the centuries from the Late Bronze Age to medieval times. The ringfort, in Irish *ráth* or *lios,* is the most numerous kind of archaeological site, with about 30–40,000 in the whole of Ireland; and in the Anascaul area they are especially numerous.

Most ringforts are circular with a single earthen rampart and ditch and rarely measure more than 200 feet (60 metres) in diameter – usually much less; but this area boasts many varieties. *Dún Chláir* in Ballinclare is a large, three-ringed fort; *Lios na Cille* at Annagap measures 400 feet (120 metres) across; and there are rectangular, square, triangular and D-shaped forts.

The impression created by the name "ringfort" can be misleading, for the vast majority were merely homesteads: few performed any more major defensive function than providing protection for man and beast from wolves and sometimes, perhaps, cattle-raiders. Insufficient excavation makes dating difficult, but most were built in and around the early Christian period. Their state of preservation varies greatly: some remain quite impressive while others have almost completely disappeared and their faint traces can only be discerned from above in evening light. In all cases soil has slipped from the walls or ramparts into the ditches, so that to imagine their original appearance it is necessary to add about five feet, on average, to both the height of the walls and the depth of the ditches.

Palisades topped the walls; and the entrances, which were sometimes stone-built, were closed with wooden doors. From the doors a plank bridge spanned the ditch. The buildings inside were of wood, wattles or stone, and the remains of these stone dwellings may sometimes still be seen. Occasionally, later buildings were erected in ringforts, such as the eighth-century church of St Martin in Lispole and the sixteenth-century castle at Rahinnane; and often they were used for many centuries as burial grounds, especially for unbaptised children. But their original function was simply as the farmsteads of the more prosperous people, in which they and their livestock could enjoy some security.

A common feature of the ringforts is the souterrain, a stone-built underground gallery roofed with large slabs, which resembles the megalithic tombs. The present state of knowledge of these underground chambers or passages is inadequate, but it is certain that they served a number of purposes, and that all or nearly all were associated with settlements, usually ringforts. Sometimes they are simply tunnelled into clay or soft rock – shales and sandstones; but in most cases there is careful and artful internal construction, whereby the passage or chamber is built with large stones set vertically and roofed with large slabs placed crossways. Chambers are approached by passages large enough for crawling on hands and knees; the entrance is sometimes narrowed by stone jambs, and the chambers are commonly about 4.5 feet (1.4 metres) high. Some chambers are larger and more elaborate and include corbelling in the stone-work, even to the extent of including underground beehive huts. In several souterrains chimneys rise from hearths marked by charcoal deposits; some are equipped with trenches to drain off water and with ventilation shafts.

Most souterrains occur within the ring of the fort, often honeycombing the entire inner area, but many go in a straight line from an opening inside the fort to another outside the rampart. Such passages were almost certainly part of the defences of the forts, and a particularly good example is at the promontory fort of *Dún Beag* in the west of the peninsula, where one can imagine defenders using it to surprise their attackers from behind. Some internal features of souterrains are clearly defensive: a stone blocking the way, with a hole slightly back from it and above from which a defender could ambush the intruder, is one of the most frequently found traps. Part of their defensive function may have been to act as a refuge for children and perhaps for valuables during an attack. But finds of objects in them have been few and inconclusive, including bronze spears and axes, ogham stones and fragments of pottery.

Many of the souterrains have enjoyed more modern use: those near the coast provided hiding places for the smugglers of the eighteenth cen-

tury; some may have served as refuges for priests and teachers in the
times of the Penal Laws and for the peasant secret societies called "tories"
and Whiteboys; and many were used both as arms caches and hide-outs
by the IRA during the War of Independence.

For centuries the ringforts, souterrains and burial mounds were regarded as the underground dwelling-places of the fairies, or *sidhe* (pronounced "shee"). Fiacc's *Hymn to Saint Patrick* asserted that "Till the
apostles came to them, darkness lay on Ireland's fold: the tribes wor-
shipped the *sidhe*"; and it is only in the last hundred years that belief in
the fairies has decisively declined. The fairies were associated with the
Tuatha Dé Danainn, and may have originated from a form of ancestor-
worship. According to early accounts the *Dé Danainn* were the fourth
wave of prehistoric invaders; they were defeated by the last colony, the
Milesians, and they dispersed to the hills and forts where they occupied
underground palaces. There they mingled with an earlier race of fairies
and were later joined by the Milesians. Some of the beliefs about them
have to do quite explicitly with respect for the ancestral dead, and it was
a respect darkened by dread.

Primarily the fairies were a central feature of folklore, and their legendary associations were of little importance. Belief in them constituted
a means of coping with the unknown, with powerful and dangerous
forces beyond control or understanding. Crop failure, blight and death
or disease in humans and livestock: people living at a subsistence level
were threatened by the inexplicable and attempted by magical means to
ward off evil consequences.

There were many superstitions about the "fairy forts". The mist of
invisibility was withdrawn from the forts at *Samhain* (Hallowe'en) – the
festival of the dead – and on the night of *Bealtaine* (May Eve/May Day)
when fairies roamed the countryside. May Day signified the start of
summer and milk production, and milk was often poured on to the
ground in ringforts and at the roots of "fairy" thorn trees as a placatory
offering. During the day of May Eve cattle were sometimes brought into
the forts: cuts were made and they were bled, some of the blood was tast-
ed and the rest poured onto the earth. Similarly, offerings of the first milk
of newly calved cows were given to the fairies. After dark on May Eve
and Hallowe'en the forts were places to be avoided.

When things went wrong the fairies were blamed: a sick cow was often thought to have been shot with flint arrowheads by the fairies; the ghosts of lost cattle were seen in forts; and when a person became suddenly ill it was thought that the true person had been snatched away to the underground world of the fairy forts and a changeling substituted. Perhaps the most persistent of the beliefs was that the fairies would avenge themselves upon anyone who tampered with their forts. In a typical example from Ballynahunt, near Anascaul, it is said that a farmer named Curran ploughed a ringfort and his mouth was turned back to the nape of his neck; the priest cured him with the aid of a prayer and a half-crown.

Lisnakilla, in open country between Annagap and the Owenascaul River, is the largest ringfort on the peninsula, with a diameter of about 400 feet (120 metres). Its name (*Lios na Cille*) derives from the fact that there was once a church within it, though hardly a trace remains. Extensive souterrains run under the surface; and when, some years ago, the wheel of a cart carrying manure went down as the roof of a souterrain collapsed, spilling the load, the manure was discarded as it would have been thought bad luck to use it. It is recalled that when the stones of the church were taken to build a pigsty many of the pigs died soon afterwards, and the man who took the stones himself died unexpectedly two years later. Other stories of the dire consequences of interfering with the fort abound, but few believe them, and even those who tell the stories laugh at them while half-believing. With the decline of superstition in recent years, some farmers have felt no reluctance to destroy ringforts, but archaeologists have appealed for their preservation.

The old church at nearby Ballynacourty has long ago disappeared leaving only a graveyard, but it was once of some importance. In 1635 Richard Boyle, the Earl of Cork – a notorious carpetbagger who obtained land and wealth after the Desmond wars by a combination of purchase, fraud and marriage – was charged before the Star Chamber with obtaining an improper lease of the parsonages of Kinard and Ballynacourty and the vicarage of Minard. From Ballynacourty the line of *Bóthar an Aifrinn*, the Mass Road, may be traced to Acres, 2.5 miles (4 kilometres) to the south, though part of it has recently been ploughed under. In the nineteenth century a Protestant church was built in the graveyard but was completely destroyed overnight. Some say that agrarian outlaws, the Whiteboys, took away all the masonry and timbers; others, that it was the work of local Catholics outraged at the appropriation of their graveyard by Protestants; but it makes, as they say, the same difference.

Between Ballynacourty and Lough Anascaul lies Knockane in Coumduff. Here at the end of the road, on the right, is a complex of remains about which archaeologists differ. Basically it consists of the somewhat submerged and poorly preserved remains of probably four graves which seem megalithic in type, and a rather interesting early Christian cross-slab. The graves have been described as megalithic tombs by some archaeologists and writers, yet are rejected as such by the Megalithic Survey of Ireland. *The Archaeological Survey of the Dingle Peninsula* suggests that because there is an early Christian cross-slab near them, the graves are probably of the same period, despite the fact that they lack the characteristics of that period, but one archaeologist suggests that it is a *ceallúnach* burial ground of a later date. The fact remains that they resemble nothing as much as megalithic cists. The cross-slab bears an unusual Greek cross decorated with a loop at the right-hand side of the upper arm which represents an abbreviated form of the *chi-rho* symbol – a stylised representation of the first two letters of Christ's name in Greek (ΧΡΙΣΤΟΣ).

In Anascaul old and new bridges cross the river side by side, and above the disused bridge the old road rises steeply to Ballinclare. The fairs here were notorious for "faction-fighting", a custom particularly associated with the early nineteenth century but which harked back to a form of symbolic tribal skirmishing associated in many cases with hilltop assemblies. Many such assemblies, and the later fairs, took place at meeting places of natural boundaries and brought together people from different sides of mountains or of major rivers, and people of different tribes and kinship groups.

A story is told of two families of the locality who were particularly renowned for fighting it out at Ballinclare Fair. A daughter and son of the opposing sides were courting and wanted to marry, and for the sake of the young couple the heads of the feuding families agreed to give up faction-fighting. At a meeting in one of their houses they each hung up the long sticks they reserved for fighting and shook hands. Come the day of the next fair, the two of them were sitting in the same house, each privately longing to be out fighting. Suddenly they heard a great clatter and looked up to see that their two sticks were beating hell out of each other on their own. Further thought was unnecessary: they took down the sticks and headed off to the fair!

The man best known for his fighting at Ballinclare was "Who's Afraid" Kennedy. Apart from its appositeness, some kind of nickname was necessary for the Kennedys, because there were so many of them that Christian names alone were not sufficient to identify the individuals of the clan; and even today after the depredations of famine and emigration there are many Kennedys in the Anascaul area who have more names than those they were christened with. Some idea of how the family spread and multiplied is given in an account in the archives of the Department of Irish Folklore at University College Dublin.

The Kennedys came from Nenagh in Tipperary. There were three brothers there: Maurice, James and Roger. Roger settled in Garfinny; Maurice settled in *Mám an Gharráin*; James was the youngest and James settled in Coumduff. They married three sisters – Mary, Cathleen and Brigid. Mary got married to Roger; Cathleen got married to Maurice; and Brigid got married to James. James had five

sons: Daniel, James, John, Maurice, Michael. Roger's descendants came to Annagap, to Ballinclare, Ballinacourty and to Anascaul. James's grandson used be fighting at Ballinclare fair. He was called "Who's Afraid". Who's Afraid's brothers, too, used be fighting at Ballinclare fair – the Currans they used be fighting against.

Just beyond the Fair Green stands an old railway cottage where the line used to cross the road. Beside the route of the line on the left of the road is the large overgrown ringfort of Doonclaur (*Dún Chláir*). About 100 feet (30 metres) in diameter, it has three large earthen banks and two fosses. Unfortunately it is very overgrown now, but even so it is possible to see some evidence of the fact that this was once an unusually substantial ringfort. Early chronicles refer to this as a "royal house" and as one of the two forts of Cú Raoi Mac Daire, the demi-god king of Caherconree. Its size and triple rings of earthen banks support the literary evidence of its importance. Local tradition has it that there is a pot of gold buried in the fort, and that the souterrain within it leads to another ringfort in fields on the other side of the road.

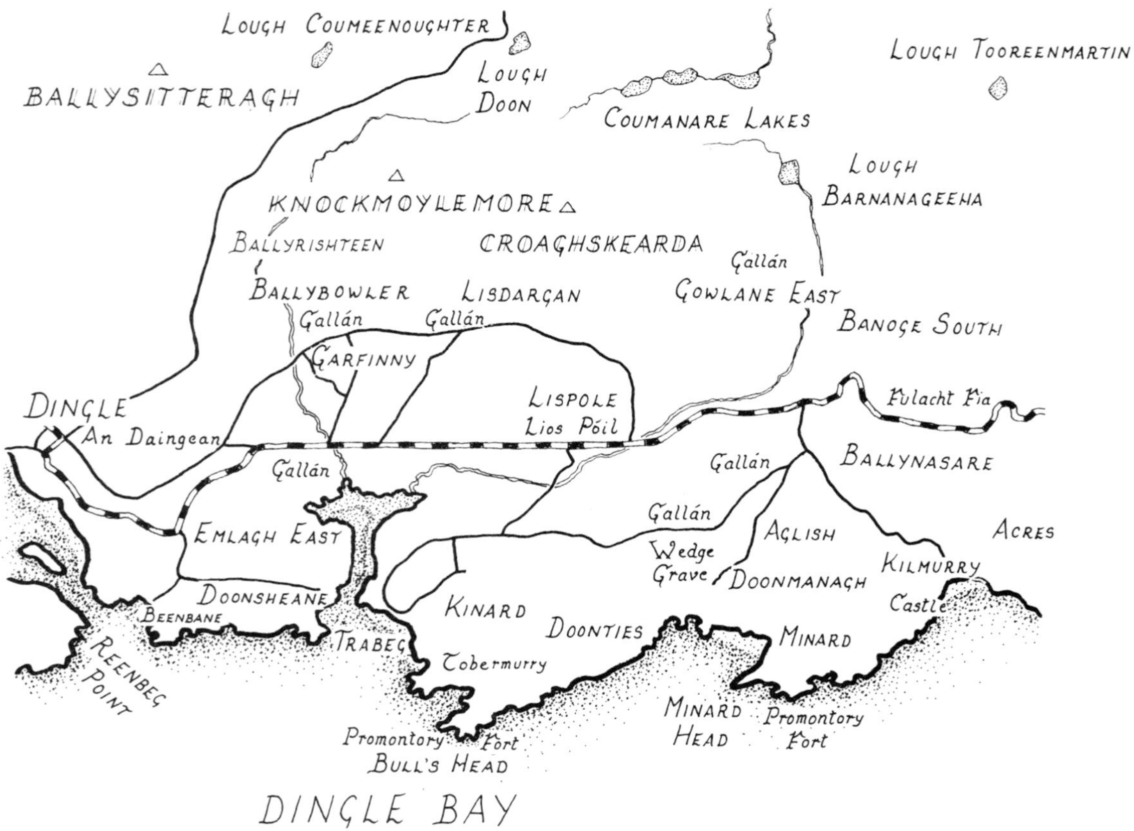
Lough Coumeenoughter
Ballysitteragh
Lough Doon
Coumanare Lakes
Lough Tooreenmartin
Lough Barnanageeha
Knockmoylemore
Ballyrishteen
Croaghskearda
Gallán
Ballybowler
Lisdargan
Gowlane East
Banoge South
Gallán
Gallán
Garfinny
Dingle
An Daingean
Lispole
Lios Póil
Fulacht Fia
Gallán
Gallán
Ballynasare
Gallán
Emlagh East
Aglish
Acres
Wedge Grave
Doonmanagh
Kilmurry
Doonsheane
Kinard
Castle
Beenbane
Doonties
Minard
Trabeg
Reenbeg Point
Tobermurry
Minard Head
Promontory Fort
Promontory Fort
Bull's Head
Dingle Bay

LISPOLE

BAILE NA SAOR (Ballinasare) means the "townland of the trades-man"; and beside the bridge, where Moriarty's forge stands below the road on the west bank of the stream, the trade of blacksmith has been carried on continuously for at least 200 years. For centuries the blacksmith was the most important craftsman in the country. While the rural economy was one of subsistence, most crafts were truly popular, as the people made almost all they needed on their farms. Some craftsmen, such as tailors and weavers, were itinerant tradesmen for there was insuf-ficient work for them to be able to stay in one small district; and many of the tinkers, or itinerants, of the present day are descended from a once substantial body of people who served even the most isolated farms with their trades.

The blacksmith enjoyed a stable and important role in the communi-ty because he offered an essential service in everyday demand, making edged tools, shoeing horses and banding cartwheels. Because he did not farm himself he was supported by a kind of tithe of the produce of the community; in particular, the heads of slaughtered animals were given to him. Mystical powers were associated with his skills, and smiths feature in many legends; he was commonly thought to be able to cure diseases and banish evil spirits, but his curse was to be avoided at all costs.

The number of forges on the peninsula has declined sharply since the introduction of the tractor and the passing of the wooden-wheeled cart. Fifty or sixty years ago 250 horses were being brought to the forge at Ballinasare Bridge from the immediate area; now there are none. The electric welder is more in use than the forge, which is rarely lit, and most of the work is in making and repairing trailers.

Situated usually at crossroads and beside rivers or streams – water was essential in the banding of wheels – the smithies were always great meeting places; information was exchanged here as people passed to the fairs at Ballinclare and Anascaul; and many would gather on wet days when there was no work to be done.

"There was a terrible lot of yarns," said the late John Moriarty. "I don't know if there was any truth at all in them. They used to say, 'Any news from the forge?' Oh, yes, it was a great place for telling lies!"

Conveniently situated across the road was a shebeen selling whiskey, which was run by a woman. As was more the rule than the exception, this was a "standing", where the drink would be sold from the house but the patrons would stand or sit in or beside the road to drink; such public display provided an invaluable propaganda target for the temperance movement. It seems to have ceased its trade at about the time the new road was built. Replacing the ford of the old road, the bridge was built in 1839 by a mason called Fitzgerald, a great-grand-uncle of Patrick Begley, who lives in a house a little above it.

Beside the stream north of the bridge are the remains of an ancient cooking place, or *fulacht fiadh*. In appearance now it is a horseshoe-shaped mound in rough, marshy land, measuring 49 feet (15 metres) north-south and 44 feet (13.5 metres) east-west; it encloses a more or less circular central mound, in which there are many burnt and fire-shattered stones.

This is a typical site of its kind, which is usually dated to the Middle to Late Bronze Age, but which spans a period from the Early Bronze Age to early historic times. Originally the cooking place centred on a trough or cooking pit enclosed in a hollow by the mound. Stones were heated in a nearby fire and then placed in the pit, where the water soon reached boiling point.

Experiments have been carried out to test the efficacy of the *fulacht fiadh* as a means of cooking. The archaeologist M.J. Kelly lit a fire beside a *fulacht fiadh* in Ballyvourney, County Cork, and heated stones in it, then placed them in the water-filled trough. Half an hour later the 100 gallons in the trough were boiling. Ten pounds (4.5 kg) of meat wrapped in straw were perfectly cooked in 3 hours and 40 minutes, during which a few additional stones were added to keep it boiling. At Dromley, also in Cork, another archaeologist, E.M. Fahy, met with similar success when he re-activated a *fulacht fiadh.*

Here at Ballinasare not only are there the remains of one *fulacht fiadh* but there were also until quite recently the remains of three more some 820 feet (250 metres) south along the bank of the river.

The name *fulacht fiadh* or, alternatively, *fulach fian* means the cooking place of the wild, or of the deer, or it means the cooking place of the Fianna. In early Irish literature it occurs in connection with the Fianna, and one gains a clear image of those roving bands of hunter-warriors setting up camp at will near some stream and creating a new cooking place or re-using an existing one. However, the numbers in which they have been found in County Cork (2000) suggest that they may have been associated with more permanent settlements. One author has suggested that they may have served primarily as sweat-houses, or primitive saunas. Only 14 have been identified on the Dingle Peninsula, but is likely that more remain unrecognised.

From Garrynadur, which houses the only pub between Anascaul and Dingle, a road is signposted to Minard Castle; a little over half a mile along the road in a field on the left is *Páirc na Fola*, "the field of blood",

a pre-Christian burial ground in which two rounded stones are inscribed with ogham writing. It is traditionally regarded as having been the site of a bloody battle in pre-history, its stones marking the graves of those who were killed.

At the end of the road Minard Castle commands Kilmurry Bay from a hillock, with a view across to the Iveragh Peninsula. This bay, with its storm beaches and its cliffs, Acres hill and the castle, was a place of undisturbed and exceptional beauty, but its appearance has been marred by recent quarrying, which has scarred the hillside. The beach of large rounded boulders is commonly known as *Béal na gCloch*, and it has many features to interest the geologist. The large stones have been piled steeply by the force of the sea concentrated by the shape of the bay; and the constant friction of the boulders against each other, assisted by sand, has given them their rounded shapes. At high tides the sound of the waves hitting the rocks and moving them is like that of repeated quarry-blasts, and as the water retreats the sound is more like the sharp crack of gunfire. In the cliffs the untrained eye can easily appreciate the form of the sandstone which was originally deposited as wind-blown sand dunes; other aspects of the geology are detailed in Ralph R. Horne's *Geological Guide to the Dingle Peninsula* (Geological Survey of Ireland, 1976).

Minard Castle, a stronghold of the Knight of Kerry, is typical of the tower-houses that were built between 1440 and 1600 as residences and fortresses of the nobility. The last of the Fitzgerald castles to be built on the peninsula, it probably dates to the late sixteenth century. Three storeys survive, but a fourth probably existed above. The first and second storeys were vaulted, but the vaults collapsed in the bombardment and explosions of 1650. At the time of the Cromwellian onslaught it was garrisoned by Walter Hussey, head of one of the leading Anglo-Norman families on the peninsula, who was resisting Cromwell's forces. Fleeing from the castle of Castlegregory in 1650, he came across the mountains, pursued by Colonels Lehunt and Sadler, and made his stand at Minard. The besiegers possessed the crucial advantage of cannon, and these they placed in the old fort of *Cathair na nAcraí* on the spur to the east. A pre-Norman ring-fort, it is very ruined, having been largely demolished earlier this century by the County Council, who used stones from it in building or repairing roads. The bombardment from the caher did extensive damage to the castle and killed many of the defenders. When those who remained alive ran out of ammunition and started using pewter for bullets, charges were placed at the four corners and their explosion was followed up with a charge in which all remaining survivors were killed. The bones of the dead lie only a small distance under the surface of the now peaceful spur.

Within living memory handball used to be played against the west wall of the castle, and a story is told locally of a young man who some sixty years ago climbed to the top of the castle to retrieve a ball and who fell from the top; he apparently picked himself up and walked home uninjured. Present-day visitors are not recommended to emulate his feat! Indeed, in recent years a substantial crack has opened up in the north wall of the castle and it is now decidedly unsafe, though it is hoped that it may be possible to carry out repairs to prevent the castle's collapse.

About 200 yards (180 metres) west of Minard Castle stands the well of St John the Baptist which is still visited. It is neatly dressed with a curved stone surround and a simple cross cut in a small stone. A community initiative in the late 1990s resulted in the erection of a decorated stone slab, the creation of a gated path and the tidying up of the surrounds of the well.

Annual devotions at wells are called patterns or patrons (*patrún* in Irish): the well is circled while decades of the rosary are said; often

pebbles are thrown in – one for each time round – but blackberries, which grow near at hand, are preferred here. The water, which was said to cure aches, used to be drunk and hands and face were washed. As with many other wells this one was reputed to contain a golden fish, the sight of which would bring good luck and ensure a cure. In the past the pattern was an occasion of great entertainment as well as devotion. Penny stalls were set up on the level triangle of grass near by, and at the top of the slip beside the coastguards' boathouse there was music and dancing into the night. But the authority of the church was brought to bear and the pattern was suppressed in all but its devotional aspect; even that, with its evidently pagan origins, was looked on with no great favour.

A particular association of the well which has contributed to the long survival of religious observance here is the legend connecting St John the Baptist with the *Corca Dhuibhne* people. This legend asserted that John the Baptist was beheaded by an Irish druid called *Mogh Roith* (the Slave of the Wheel) from Valentia Island on the other side of Dingle Bay, and prophesied that the Irish people – and especially the *Corca Dhuibhne* – would be called upon to pay for the crime at a date when certain time divisions coincided. In 1096 it was thought that the appointed time was approaching, and Ireland was seized with a panic, similar to the millenialist hysteria that had gripped many in Europe a century before. Rigorous fasting and prayer were undertaken, and it is probably from this date that the well derived its importance, along with many others dedicated to St John the Baptist. On the hill above the well little remains of the early church of St Mary (*Cill Mhuire*, or Kilmurry); some of its stones were used in the construction of nearby farm buildings. Recently the well itself inspired a fine poem, "An bhábóg bhriste", by Nuala Ní Dhomhnaill (*Féar Suaithinseach*, 1984).

Customs such as patterns at holy wells and the oral tradition of story and song remained strong on the Dingle Peninsula until the intervention of the clergy, radio, television, motor cars and the building of new houses in isolation rather than in clusters combined to eliminate opportunities – or, indeed, any popular wish – for their maintenance. That they lasted longer here was a consequence of slow economic development. In Minard, as in some other parts, songs which were popular forty years ago are fading from memory. One such song is a "Skellig List" – a form of satire directed at unmarried people. On the island of Skellig Michael the old Julian calendar was still observed long after it had been replaced elsewhere; this meant that Lent was later there, and so offered an imagined extension of the marrying season. The composer of the "List" places the unmarried adults of the neighbourhood on board a boat sailing from Bealacoon in West Minard to the Skellig:

> The travellers for the Skelligs soon were all assembling here,
> Like swallows in the summertime they flocked from everywhere:
> Old bald and hairy gentlemen you'd see in twos and threes
> And some bobbed and shingled damsels with their clothes above
>   their knees.

And in fourteen verses full of names, the "marriage-shy" people of the parish are lampooned.

At a time when soap operas and videos were unthought of and poverty made visits to the pub rare enough, incidents were seized upon to provide entertainment and songs were composed to exploit and prolong their entertainment value. Another song from Minard is "The Barrell of Rum", which opens:

> 'Tis long we will remember the year of Forty-Three;
> A storm it was raging in the month of January;
> The twenty-fifth day of that month at three o'clock that day
> A barrell was seen floating on the waves of Dingle Bay.

And it goes on to celebrate how the rum was saved by local people who "drank enough and they all got tough, you could see them roll and fall".

A ROAD leads towards Aglish from the Minard-Garrynadur road; and from it another road leads past a quarry along the hill ridge on which a transmission mast stands; less than a quarter of a mile west, on the right of this road, is the split standing stone of *An Ghráig*. The standing part is 12 feet (3.5 metres) high while the detached part lies at an angle of 45 degrees.

Half a mile along the road from the stone at *Gráig* a muddy boreen leads to the left, and on the small hill above stands the wedge grave of

Púicín an Chairn. The same in type as the graves at Maumnahaltora, it is unusual for the fact that some of the cairn of smaller, loose stones that originally covered it is still in place. The remains of small, low, curving walls radiate from the grave.

There is a fine view from *Púicín an Chairn* of the land between Doonmanagh and Minard Head and of the coastline with its cliffs, inlets and jutting headlands. Behind Minard Head is Minard promontory fort, the most easterly of the many defended headlands that thrust into the sea on the south coast of the peninsula. The promontory is 180 feet (55 metres) long and very narrow at about 30 feet (9 metres) wide. Its 16 metres long fosse is 2.75 metres deep and it has an inner wall, within which is what was probably a guard-chamber. Another promontory fort lies west of Minard Head, three-eighths of a mile from the end of the road at Bealacoon. It possesses the clear characteristic of the promontory having been artificially narrowed at the neck, inside which an earthen rampart provides further defence.

The entire coastline in this area fascinates with its variety of rock shapes, colours and formations, but walkers approach cliffs at their peril – erosion by pounding seas, gales and rain causes continual slippages and occasional substantial falls of the softer rocks.

From *Púicín an Chairn* the road continues west to Ardamore; and at a farmhouse about half a mile on a cross-slab was found, probably of the

eighth century, with an elegant Greek cross in a round panel. Discovered by a farmer in 1978, an excavation found nothing else at the site and it is thought that it may have been brought there at some time from an early Christian settlement elsewhere. The cross-slab may now be seen at the Heritage Centre in Ballyferriter. At the end of the bohareen that runs through the farm is an alignment of three stones 25 feet (7.5 metres) long; a fourth stone, an outlier, stands 197 feet (60 metres) to the north-east. The tallest of the stones is 10 feet (3 metres) high and the outlier is decorated on its north-east face with rock art and a cup-and-two circles in its centre. The alignment is orientated on the setting sun at the winter solstice, and there may have been a boulder dolmen, since destroyed, associated with it.

Less than half a mile along the road from the farmhouse, just beyond a stream, there is a ringfort on the right. *Áth an Charbaill* ringfort is mostly destroyed but it possesses an interesting, L-shaped souterrain, in the construction of which three ogham stones and a cross-slab were re-used. Across the road in a field lies a large stone decorated with rock art. Part of it is concealed by the field wall, but on the visible area of the stone the main features are several incised cup shapes surrounded by concentric circles. There are 30 plain cup-marks, a cup-and-radial line, and 8 cup-marks enclosed by between one and three concentric circles. This type of design is found in Ireland and in highland areas of Britain, and is probably related to similar scribings in Spain; the most notable examples of this essentially Bronze Age art are at Newgrange in Ireland and in the Clava Tombs on the Moray Firth in Scotland. A few fields to the west of the stone stands the cashel called *Lios an Anacail* (confusingly anglicised to Lissonenakilla), a name which suggests that it may have been constructed for a particular defensive purpose rather than just as a farmstead. The stone wall of the cashel is about 10 feet (3 metres) wide and 3 feet (1 metre) high internally; in the centre of the enclosure is a collapsed *clochán*.

A mile to the west and a quarter of a mile south from a staggered crossroads is Kinard, birthplace of Thomas Ashe, the leader of the Irish Republican Brotherhood who died on hunger strike in 1917. His house still stands at the southern end of a cluster of houses, and near by a monument to him was erected in 1985 and unveiled by Sean McBride, the former chief-of-staff of the IRA and winner of both the Nobel and Lenin

Peace Prizes. Here Ashe's playing of the bagpipes, for which he was also well known nationally, is remembered: on Sunday evenings he would play his music sitting on the craggy summit of the hill above his home.

His greatest moment came in 1916 when he commanded the most successful military action outside Dublin, at Ashbourne in County Meath. He was condemned to death but reprieved; and he became leader of the Irish Republican Brotherhood. In September 1917 he was one of eighty-four republican prisoners in Mountjoy Prison who demanded political prisoner status and when it was denied went on hunger strike after destroying everything in their cells. His death after forcible feeding by the prison authorities proved a turning point in rallying mass support behind the demand not only for political status – which was conceded soon afterwards – but for national independence. Twenty thousand people followed his coffin to Dublin's Glasnevin cemetery, where he was buried with republican military honours, and many thousands more lined the streets.

Another native of Kinard, and a great-grand-uncle of Thomas Ashe, was a well-known smuggler by the name of Sean Mór Griffin. As a result of England's crippling economic domination, the development of an Irish middle class was forced to take some unusual twists and turns; and what would have been the normal trade of merchants in independent countries took the form of smuggling here. The small strand below Kinard, Trabeg, is where the contraband was brought in. It is a pleasant spot on a fine day and a dramatic one in stormy weather; the beach can be dangerous for swimming at times. From the road beside the strand there is an excellent view of the large rampart of *Dún Sían* promontory fort, the "fort of the fairies".

There are in reality two promontory forts, Doonmore and Dunbeg – Dunbeg being a small, and now inaccessible projection from the much larger Doonmore. The earthen bank at the neck of the promontory stands 22 feet (6.6 metres) high above the base of the ditch, or fosse, and when one considers that both the bank has eroded and the fosse has filled in, these must have been impressive defences in their day. A stone wall 5 feet (1.5 metres) wide is partially preserved along the top of the bank.

In nearby Kinard East a large boulder in a field is richly decorated with rock art, featuring cup-and-two circles, gapped circles, radial lines and satellite cups.

In the graveyard close by are two ogham stones, one of which stands upright in the ground near the western side of the graveyard and is decorated with an unusual cross in the form of a rectangle divided into four quadrants, the upper two of which are further subdivided. Its ogham inscription reads: MARIAN. The other ogham stone lies in the north-west part of the graveyard, and it is inscribed: SANGTI LLOTETI AVI SRUSA. There is also a small *bullán* stone with a single depression.

No trace remains of the church that once stood here, but the fact that there are ogham stones and a *bullán* on the site suggests that this was once an early Christian settlement. Subsequently there was a parish church here, which was mentioned in the Papal Taxation List (1302–07) for the Diocese of Ardfert. In disrepair in 1458, it was probably restored in the fifteenth or sixteenth century.

Three wells lie a little to the west of the graveyard. The story is told that Saint Fíonáin and Saint Michael landed at nearby Trabeg from the island of Skellig Michael; the Virgin Mary appeared to them out of the fog that blanketed the coast and three wells opened at their feet. In 1918 *Tobar Mhuire* and *Tobar Fhíonáin* were edified as a thanksgiving for their waters having supposedly cured many people during the epidemic of influenza that swept through all of Europe at the end of the war. They are still visited and are two of the few wells on the peninsula to be dressed by stone surrounds and a statue. *Tobar Fhíonáin* is visited on February 12th when a pattern used to be held, *Tobar Mhuire* on February 2nd, March 25th, August 15th and December 8th, and *Tobar Mhichíl* used to be visited on September 29th.

About three-quarters of a mile from *Tobar Mhuire* as the crow flies – but a longer walk over rough hillside – is the most substantial of all the promontory forts on the coast of *Corca Dhuibhne*, at Bull's Head. Extraordinarily, this was only recognised as a fort as late as 1978, and yet its large defensive wall is visible from several miles away. A 656 feet (200 metres) long defensive wall, or series of walls, incorporating a large rock outcrop, cuts across the neck of the promontory, overloooking the landward approach. Within this enclosure is an area of about 1150 feet (350 metres) by 1050 feet (320 metres) which mostly consists of steeply sloping ground rising from cliffs. The defences of the fort have suffered considerable collapse and interference, and several sheepfolds have been built into their western end. Within the enclosure are at least 14 hut-sites, and a series of about 75 low, circular depressions which are between 3 feet (1 metre) and 16 feet (5 metres) in diameter. They encircle the three seaward sides of the upper slopes of the promontory and they do not appear to be hut-sites, but what they are, or were, no one seems to know.

The best time to visit Bull's Head is during the winter for bracken grows on all but the most exposed parts of the promontory, covering the enigmatic evidence. The slopes from the peak of 376 feet (115 metres) are steep and should be treated with extreme caution. North-east of the promontory are ruined *clocháin*, further signs that this bleak and deserted area was once the scene of some activity.

OUR ROUTE has at this stage taken a long detour from the main road – a detour taking in Minard, Ardamore and Kinard. The main road continues from where we left it in Garrynadur to the village of Lispole, passing a school, community hall and sports field. Anyone walking or cycling from Garrynadur to Lispole will find the old road more pleasant: it runs parallel with the main road. The church in Lispole was built in 1867 and its stone, like that of St Mary's in Dingle, was quarried at Kilmurry Bay. The stone and metal railway bridge still stands in clear view, and on the left-hand side of the road is a memorial to those who died in the Lispole Ambush when the IRA attacked the British forces in the War of Independence. One of those killed was a brother of Thomas Ashe of Kinard.

The road bridge in Lispole was known as "the Poteen Bridge", and the illegal spirit must have been distilled around here. However, in general the peninsula has very little tradition of poteen – certainly compared with some other parts of Ireland – and this is probably because of an abundance of smuggled spirits in the eighteenth and nineteenth centuries.

One can detour off the main road and explore the countryside northwest of here, winding up eventually on the old road to Dingle. Immediately after the bridge in Lispole turn right. At a crossroads turn left and a little less than 200 yards (180 metres) further on there is a gateway on the left. Two fields below here is St Martin's, a late eighth century church built inside a ringfort and now much ruined. Within the large oval enclosure are the foundations of several rectangular house sites.

The ruins of Templemartin are of an early church which was extended eastwards in the fifteenth or sixteenth century.

Returning to the crossroads and turning left, in Gowlin the remains of an old road lead off to the right. For the walker who likes to ramble over rough ground there is a walk here across the boulder-strewn foot of the mountains – some of the boulders have been used as *gallán* and there is an extensive system of pre-bog walls – and up the quite gentle slope to where Lough Barnanageeha sits beneath steep cliffs and there is a track leading up into the Windy Gap.

In Gowlin is an interesting souterrain called *Staighre Chaitlín* (Kathleen's stairs). There are three chambers in the souterrain and a story is told of buried treasure here. A local man dreamed that there was treasure on Limerick Bridge, so he travelled by horse or donkey to Limerick and approached the bridge. At the middle of its span he met a man leaning over the parapet and joined him in his silent contemplation of the river. They spoke then, and the second man revealed that he, too, had had a dream about treasure, and in his dream the treasure had been buried at a place called *Staighre Chaitlín*, but he knew of no place by that name. The Kerryman, being a canny fellow, said nothing but returned home to Gowlin where he entered *Staighre Chaitlín* and found the treasure.

The road to the left in Gowlin leads to a lamb fattening unit and towards Lisdargan. Near by, below the road, is Lisnarahardia, and there are many other ringforts in this fertile segment of land between Gowlin and Garfinny. There are also several standing stones, one of which is visible just inside the hedge on the right-hand side of the road as it approaches Garfinny.

At the river in Garfinny, the road drops down to a bridge, to the right of which is a ford, while to the left is an old bridge, known as the "rainbow bridge". It is a very slender pack-horse bridge, which has recently been cleaned and restored, and its apparently simple elegance is the product of a sophisticated understanding of structure and water-flow. Although local tradition has it that the English army of Lord Grey of Wilton marched over it en route to the *Dún an Óir* massacre in 1580, the arch of the bridge is a nineteenth-century reconstruction. A detailed description can be found in *Irish Stone Bridges: History and Heritage* (1991) by Peter O'Keeffe and Tom Simington. The road continues past Garfinny graveyard and swings around the hill and into Dingle via John Street.

Taking the straight main road from Lispole to Dingle it can be interesting to observe as you travel along the road the changing shape of the hills – particularly of Croaghskearda. Also, in the townland of Ballineesteenig, on the left-hand side of the road beside a farmhouse and in front of a new bungalow, stands perhaps the finest of the many standing stones on the peninsula.

Just after the road swings to the left after the long straight stretch, the headland of Bull's Head stands out clearly to the south-east. On a clear day the wall cutting across the neck of the peninsula is quite visible. The road swings to the right again and passes the large field in which the Dingle Races are held.

It is not the most sophisticated racecourse in Ireland, but the flapper races held in mid-August every year are lively and enjoyable. Travellers – also known as tinkers or itinerants – set up stalls and swings; there is no lack of bookies; and horses are brought from as far away as County Donegal and Wales. Stories abound of horses being entered under false names, of riders holding back mounts not intended to win, and of all kinds of rows and goings-on; whether there is an iota of truth in such stories or not, they seem to be an essential ingredient of the event and to

be relished in the best of humour. As the much-loved newspaper columnist, Con Houlihan, has written:

> In the famous field at Ballintaggart you will see swinging-boats and merry-go-rounds and shooting stalls and a bar constructed of planks and barrels and canvas, not to mention the wheel of fortune where the prizes include holy pictures and sets of ware and very alarming clocks.
>
> You will see horses too – a fact which is hardly surprising when you consider the prize-money... And if you are a regular patron of the flapper circuit, the occasional horse will wink at you as he is led around in the parade ring.

SIMPLE PLEASURES

SIMPLE PLEASURES
The Mall, Dingle
Tel/Fax: 066 9151224

- *Collectors Teddy Bears*
  by Barbara-Ann
  - *Memorabilia*
  - *Art Gallery*
  - *Jewellery*
  - *Porcelain Pieces*
  - *Fine Prints*
  - *Antique Linen*

Proprietors: Julie & Michael Hennessy

THE OLD DANCE HALL ANTIQUES

• *House Furnishings* • *Gifts* • *Collectables & Effects*

Tel/Fax 066 9157411   Mobile 087 2261415

Four miles from Dingle on the Dingle-Tralee road

KILCOOLY
Cráilí
BALLINLOGHIG
LOUGH NAMNA
KILMALKEDAR
REENCONNELL
CAHERDARGAN
LOUGH GAL
CLOGHAREE
LOUGH
CONNOR HILL
LOUGH DOON
GLIN
BALLYSITTERAGH
LOUGH
COUMEENOUGHTER
SLIEVANEA
BALLYNANA
KNOCKMOYLEMORE
BALLYHEABOUGHT
BALLYRISHTEEN
CROAGHSKEARDA
KNOCKAVROGEEN
Templemanaghan
BALLYBOWLER
LISDARGAN
Gallán
Gallán
KNOCKNAHORAN
BALLYMOREREAGH
KILFOUNTAIN
GARFINNY
MILLTOWN
CAHERBOSHINA
DINGLE
Gallán
An Daingean
LISPOLE
EMLAGH
DINGLE
HARBOUR
EAST
BALLINTAGGART
BURNHAM
Ogham Stones
DOONSHEANE
Promontory
Fort
BALLYMACADOYLE
HILL
EASK
Tower
KINARD
DOONTIES
REENBEG POINT
BEENBANE HEAD
TRABEG
Promontory
Fort
Tobermurry
Promontory
Fort
DINGLE BAY
Promontory
Fort
BULL'S HEAD

DINGLE TOWN

OUNTAINS AT ITS back, Dingle faces comfortably on to a sheltered harbour, solid houses presenting coloured fronts to the sea. From level ground at Strand Street on the harbour's edge and at the Mall beside the Dingle River, three main streets rise: Green Street, John Street and Main Street. About 1400 people live in Dingle, but it serves the larger population of the surrounding countryside, and in the summer months it caters for many thousands of visitors.

Fishing and farming have long been the major industries, but tourism has become an increasingly important business in the town, particularly since the filming of *Ryan's Daughter* in the area in 1969, and craft shops and restaurants have sprung up all over the town. The amount of tourist accommodation available increased enormously in the late 1980s and the 1990s.

As a market town and fishing port, Dingle has long been well supplied with pubs; in recent years the number has hovered around fifty-two, and the variety is almost as great as the number. There are large, modern pubs and pubs so small that five's a crowd; one that sells wellingtons and leather belts, another that sells sheets and blankets and another that sells everything from beds and bicycles to creosote and fertiliser. Much of the social life of the town revolves around pubs: during the winter there are card games and quizzes. In the summer the emphasis is on tourist customers, and Irish music is played almost every night in about ten pubs.

For the visitor, exploring the pubs of Dingle can be an adventure and an entertainment in itself. Much depends on luck, of course, but it is generally not difficult to get into conversation and to discover the meaning of the Irish term "crack", which has nothing to do with illicit substances and all to do with enjoying yourself and enjoying good company.

For visitors based in Dingle there is a considerafble variety of things to do, and in planning the day a key consideration will be the weather. The west coast gets a fair amount of rain, but summer showers are usually just that and often pass very quickly. If you are unlucky it may be necessary to adopt the philosophically positive Kerry approach: if it is raining, you say it's a "soft day".

Dingle is an excellent centre from which to explore the surrounding countryside on foot, and there are pleasant walks to be made in almost every direction. In the town there are craft shops which can be comfortably browsed in whatever the weather.

On the Mail Road, which enters the town from the east, is the Gaelic football pitch, where visitors may like to see a match on a Sunday afternoon. Posters around the town proclaim various entertainments: occasionally there are plays, but traditional music flourishes best of all here, and there are almost nightly sessions in O'Flaherty's in Bridge Street, An Droichead Beag and the Dingle Pub in Main Street, Máire de Barra's, the Marina Bar and Murphy's in Strand Street, and less frequently in other venues. At the Hillgrove Hotel there are various musical events, including discos, with set-dancing currently every Thursday,

and the Skellig hotel features traditional music and dance and occasional concerts.

The town is renowned for its restaurants which provide excellent seafood and French cuisine, but there are also plenty of other restaurants, pubs and cafés offering a variety of menus. During the summer visitors wanting to eat in the more upmarket restaurants are advised to go early for their meals. Tipping is at the discretion of the customer, but ten per cent is common.

In the craft shops the best value to be found is in high quality hand-made products, such as tweed and woollen clothing, leather goods, jewellery, turned wood and pottery. Most if not all of the shops are well used to packing and shipping their goods.

In shopping for everyday requirements, visitors cannot expect to find the range of products available in large city stores; but, that said, there is a very respectable range for a town the size of Dingle. There are three supermarkets, a host of butchers, and several small general grocers.

Advice and information about accommodation in Dingle can be readily obtained at the Tourist Office at the head of the pier. There are three hotels in the town – Benner's, the Hillgrove and the Skellig – and several hostels of varying size in and around the town; there are guesthouses and bed-and-breakfast places in almost every street, and some apartments for rent. During the summer months pressure on accommodation can be considerable and anyone arriving on spec should not leave it late to go looking.

THE IMMEDIATE surroundings of the town offer a variety of walks of different lengths. The one most favoured by local people is out along the harbour's edge, by "the banks"; and it has the distinct advantage of leading to two safe places for bathing. Opposite Moran's Garage is Cooleen, with its row of cottages. At the end of this short road is a long single-storey building which houses a variety of companies; bear right at the gateway and take the path right by the water's edge; this goes down some steps at the boathouse and up again and continues along the edge of the harbour and past the Skellig Hotel, built on the site of a coastguard station which was burnt down in 1922 during the Civil War. The area in front of the hotel was the scene in 1991/92 of protest demonstrations, as Dingle people fought a campaign to prevent the privatisation of the foreshore and the creation of a 350-berth marina together with a village of holiday houses and onshore facilities for the marina. Although a government-appointed tribunal found in favour of granting a license for the project, the determined opposition of Dingle's citizens to what they perceived as an entirely inappropriate development resulted in the planned marina's being abandoned.

Continuing along the shoreline, one comes to Hussey's Folly, a tower built during the Famine of the 1840s, which was used shortly after that as a customs watchtower.

Below and on the far side of the tower is Slaudeen, a small bathing place favoured by people from the town. Further on is the lighthouse, and about 200 yards before it is a cave called Nancy Brown's Parlour. The fanciful local belief is that the cave extends back into Dingle and surfaces at the old presbytery.

In the sea here at the harbour's mouth fishermen first began in 1983 to notice that a dolphin was persistently following their boats. Initially they had paid little attention, because schools of dolphins pass along the coast quite frequently, but soon they realised that one particular bottle-nosed dolphin had apparently taken up residence. A couple of years later some sub-aqua divers established a habit of diving here and trying to get close to the dolphin. Gradually he began to come closer, then to play games with them, and after a while word began to spread about him.

By 1987 one 12-seater boat was making a regular business of bringing people out to see the dolphin, who had by now been christened "Fungie", and at Christmas that year he made his first appearance on Irish television. In 1988 Horace Dobbs's television documentary called *The Dolphin's Touch* was shown on ITV, and soon Fungie was an international celebrity, provoking a tourist boom in Dingle. By 1991 some fifteen boats of varying sizes were regularly taking visitors on trips to see the dolphin at the harbour's mouth.

There is a path along the top of the cliff which, after passing the lighthouse (built in 1886), leads to Beenbane Strand, a safe bathing place a mile further on. On Beenbane Head a pile of stones is all that remains of another beacon, which was similar to the beacon at Eask that dominates the southern skyline from Dingle. West of the site of the signal station is the promontory fort of Beenbane, with its clearly defined bank and shallow fosse. The cliffs around Beenbane are very dramatic and the walker can expect to see fulmars, choughs and shelduck here.

At any stage in the walk one can turn back to Dingle on the same route, but a pleasant longer walk, which takes four to five hours in all from Dingle, is to continue along the cliff to Doonsheane and back to Dingle via Ballintaggart.

Doonsheane – *Dún Sían* – the fort of the fairies – is a promontory fort with high earthen ramparts cutting across the neck of the promontory. From the strand below, a river runs inland and after half a mile there is a point. To the left along the Short Strand here there is a rock slab known as the Priest's Stone, which is an ogham stone, the first to be discovered. It was identified by Edward Lluyd, a Welsh antiquarian, in the early eighteenth century; its inscription reads: "Bruscus son of Caliacus", and it also bears a cross.

A bohareen leads from the stone through the village of Doonsheane; beyond the village another bohareen leads off to the right and three fields beyond the junction the hillock of Ballintaggart burial ground is visible.

Enclosed within a stone wall and a low earthen bank, this *ceallúnach*, or burial ground, is important for its ogham stones. Rounded stones of the kind found at Kilmurry Bay beside Minard Castle are marked with ogham inscriptions and some also with crosses. Ogham writing originated in Ireland in about the fourth century AD as a means of

inscribing tombstones and is similar to runic script, consisting of a series of lines grouped and related to a keyline, which is often the edge of an angular stone. It may have been in use earlier as an alphabet or form of writing notched on sticks, and it has been suggested that it came from Gaul in the first century BC. About 300 ogham stones have been identified in Ireland, and another 60 in areas of Irish influence in Britain; and the largest concentration of finds has been in the territory peopled by the *Corca Dhuibhne*, on the Dingle and Iveragh Peninsulas.

The alphabet is made up of twenty main letters which divide neatly into four groups of five, and it is based on the Roman alphabet. It is a very cumbersome form of writing and the inscriptions are of names, often indicating ancestry and the tribal deity of the person commemorated. Two of the stones at Ballintaggart include the name Dovinnias, a version of Duibhne, the goddess or original ancestress of the *Corca Dhuibhne*. There are nine ogham stones here, arranged in a circle within the enclosure of the *ceallúnach*. All were brought from fields in the immediate vicinity.

Resuming the walk, continue on the road from Doonsheane village and take the first right, which leads to the main road. Here one can return to Dingle by the main road, but it is more interesting to head almost immediately uphill along a bohareen and bear left. At the top, a road skirts the hill, and this is the old road into Dingle. Inside the bend at the far side of the road is a fine ringfort. It is unusual in having a raised interior inside its exterior fosse, enclosing bank and interior fosse. Trees now grow on the bank which encloses a sub-circular area measuring between 95 feet (29 metres) and 120 feet (36.5 metres). The road leads down into Dingle and offers an excellent view of the town from above.

Some people like to stretch their legs, but only briefly. Apart from circling the town – up Main Street, down to Milltown and back to Strand Street – the best short walk is undoubtedly up Knockahoran. The Hill of the Cairn, *Cnoc an Chairn*, it has a pile of stones on its modest summit, from which there is an excellent view of the harbour, the town, Burnham and, on a clear day, the Iveragh Peninsula. Like many of the hills in the area, it is richly colourful in autumn, purple heather combining with yellow gorse. The hill is the end of a mountain ridge, and a track below the summit provides an even surface for walking further up the ridge.

WITH ITS tower, its cliffs and its dramatically situated promontory fort, Eask is a memorable place to visit. Directly across the harbour and clearly visible from the town, it can be approached by car, motorbike or bicycle, or one can walk the whole way there and back, a distance of about ten miles.

To walk it, leave town by Milltown Bridge, beside which are the remains of the old mill and race, one of the last water-powered mills in Ireland. Uphill, on the Slea Head road, there is a cemetery on the left, and in a field on the right, only slightly further on, is an ancient burial ground with a complex of megaliths. Now in the front garden of a new house stands a *gallán* known as the "Milestone", or *Gallán na Cille Brice*. About 70 metres north-east there is a pair of *gallán* known as the "Gates of Glory", the taller of which now lies prostrate, and the smaller of which is broken. About 50 metres south of the "Gates of Glory" and 20 metres from the "Milestone" is a pair of prostrate stones, one of which is decorated with 8 cup-and-circles and about 18 single cup marks; there are also a number of radial lines. The final stone in this complex of megalithic monuments is a *gallán* on the other side of the road, some 250 metres south-southwest of the "Milestone".

The road bears left shortly and then enters a wooded area at Burnham. A left turn here, signposted, leads to Reenbeg and *Coláiste Íde*. English settlers called Mullins bought land here in 1666, later changing their

name to de Moleyns and being granted, in 1800, the title of Viscounts of Ventry. They built a large house on the site of a sixteenth-century castle of the Rice family and became owners of a large proportion of the Dingle Peninsula, as well as land in Killorglin. They supplied captains of the militia and, in the nineteenth century, gave active support to the efforts to convert Catholics to Protestantism. The Burnham Peninsula consisted of a series of villages and the population included both farmers and fishermen; however, Lord Ventry evicted them (Cooleen in Dingle and Coumaleague in Ventry are two of the places they were moved to) and developed the area as his own estate. Early this century Lord Ventry sold his property to the government and moved to England. The land-lords' house became the convent boarding school of *Coláiste Íde*. In the grounds of the college there is a group of ogham stones, brought here from the surrounding countryside.

The grounds were planted with a number of exotic plants, which grow well in the warm, wet climate here, and vigorous growths of bamboo can be seen. In the open countryside the hill on the right is Ballymacadoyle Hill, known in the sixteenth century as Harperstown after a notable family of harpers that lived here. Another resident of the area was Padraig Ó Siochfradha, scholar, author and local historian, who wrote down much of the lore of placenames as it existed nearly a hundred years ago.

Beyond Ballymacadoyle is Eask, which is easy to climb up to from the road below. The tower of solid stone with a wooden hand projecting from it and pointing to the blind harbour's mouth, was built to provide work during the Famine, at the instigation of the Reverend Charles Gayer, leader of the Protestant attempts to win converts. The concrete remains beside it are of a look-out post from World War II – or, as it was known in Ireland, "the Emergency". There is a magnificent view from here of the expanse of Dingle Bay, the Iveragh Peninsula, Dingle town nestling below the mountains, and the country and coastline to the east.

The cliffs are steep on the far side of Eask Tower, but to the right a promontory projects out from the cliffs at a height of around 500 feet (152 metres) above sea level. The neck is cut across by a series of staggered earthen ramparts and ditches, and also by the remains of a stone wall, the line of which may clearly be seen extending down the steep sides of the promontory to the water's edge. The natural rock formation makes of the promontory a series of platforms, reminiscent of the many different levels on a warship. People with a poor head for heights are advised not to venture across the narrow neck of the promontory. Low down at the seaward side are the remains of stone dwellings, and a group of upright slabs on this southern side may be the remains of *Relig an Dúna*, a burial ground.

MANY EXCURSIONS can be made from Dingle into the surrounding countryside, and the starting point for many of them is Milltown Bridge at the west of the town. The road that leads directly north from the town side of the bridge leads eventually to Brandon Creek and the Feohanagh area. But first it passes through Ballynabooly and Ballyheabought. In this second townland, near the road on the right hand side, is a ringfort with the remains of two *clocháin* and the ruins of a rectangular building. Originally this ringfort had two banks and two fosses, but the outer bank and fosse were levelled and the inner fosses have been filled with debris. However, the inner bank, which is 12 to 14 feet (3.5 to 4 metres) thick, shows a good example of dry-stone masonry facing and now stands about 6 feet (1.75 metres) high.

Further along this same road, at a crossroads three miles (five kilometers) from Milltown Bridge, the turn to the left leads to

Reenconnell. On the right is a farmhouse and in a field directly behind it is an early Christian stone cross within a rectangular enclosure. Set now in a concreted base, the cross, although very weathered, bears the clear inscription of two straight lines and two concentric circles at the heart of the cross.

Another early Christian settlement, at Kilfountain, is reached by returning to Milltown Bridge, crossing it and taking the first turn right along the long, straight road known as the *bóthar fada*. A mile and a quarter along the road is a small bridge; just before it a green track leads off to the right towards farm buildings, beyond which on the left is the Kifountain settlement. It is a very ruined site, with the remains of an oratory, *clocháin*, an enclosure wall and a *bullán*, but it is notable for its cross-slab. Slender and strangely elegant, this bears a Greek cross with a

circle and a formalised representation of *chi-rho*, the first letters of Christ's name in Greek; and inscribed on it vertically is the name of the founder of the settlement, Finten.

The hill above Kilfountain is *Cnoc an Bhrugín*, or Knockavrogeen, the hill of the small mansion, which has also been translated as the hill of the palace. Its name may have some connection with the five ringforts which are strung like the pearls of a necklace around the south and east slopes of the hill, suggesting that a particularly substantial local family lived here in the early Christian period. There are six ringforts in all on Knockavrogeen and most of them measure about 30 metres in diameter, though the largest is 36 metres and the smallest 24 metres, and two of them are double-banked.

Many other excursions can be made from Dingle, and the most popular of these is undoubtedly the trip around Slea Head to the west. The roads provide for journeys which encircle parts of the countryside and wind up back in Dingle again: there is the route around Slea Head and back via Dunquin and Ventry, or one can go further, continuing north from Dunquin to Ballyferriter; from Ballyferriter one has the option of continuing north again and taking in the whole north-western region including Brandon Creek, or of returning to Dingle via either Ballynana or Ventry.

O' Flaherty's Bar

Bridge Street,
Dingle

Togha ceoil agus rogha
díghe ar fáil anseo

FACING THE FUTURE.

FREE TO CHOOSE THE BEST.

Freedom! Leaving school is challenging, but confusing.

But whether you're starting work or going on to college, AIB can help. At your local AIB Bank Branch the Student Officer will be glad to give you advice on how to manage your finances.

And, when you open an account with AIB, we'll give you a free book of special discount vouchers for outlets nationwide.

So, what are you waiting for? Call AIB today and we'll help you make the most of your freedom.

AIB
Bank

You bring out the best in us

Main Street, Dingle, Co. Kerry   Tel: (066) 9151400 Fax (066) 9151861

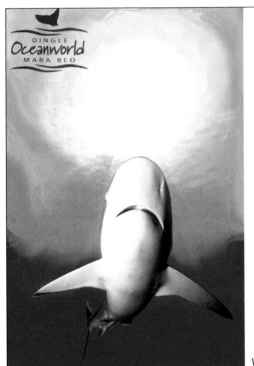

DINGLE TOWN

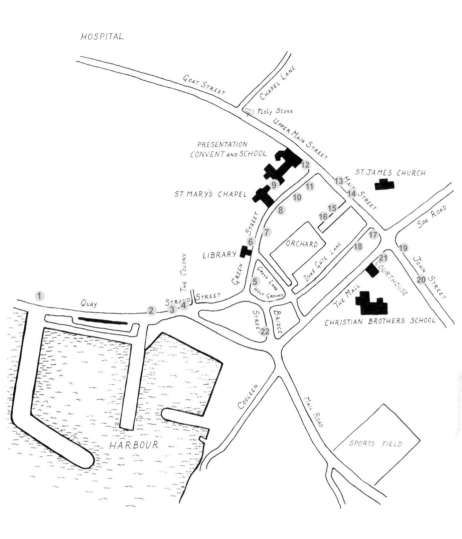

Map of Advertisers

THE HISTORIC TOWN

NOBODY KNOWS WHEN Dingle first became a centre of population. Some people mention the fact that Queen Elizabeth I of England announced, in 1585, her intention of granting the town a charter, and suggest that Dingle is therefore four hundred years old. However, the place was populated for a good deal more than four hundred years before Queen Bess took an interest.

The proper name for the town is *Daingean Uí Chúis*, O'Cush's fortress. The fact that there is no record of the name O'Cush has led to a suggestion that the name is a corruption of Hussey, or Huysse, a Flemish family which came to the area in the thirteenth century. In a document of 1290 the name of the town is given as Dengynhuysse.

When the Norman settlers arrived in the thirteenth century they quickly set about developing Dingle as a very substantial trading port. Butter, wool, hides, fish and meat were exported, and coal, salt, clothes and wine were imported. By the fourteenth century it was a major Irish centre of trade, particularly with Spain and France. Merchants' houses were built here of Spanish design, and small decorated stones set into the outside walls of houses in Green Street come from this period of Spanish influence.

The Spanish role went beyond trade, for Spanish troops combined with Irish rebel forces against the English in 1580, during what were known as the Desmond Wars. Their intervention was tragically unsuccessful and almost the entire Spanish and Papal Italian force was massacred by the English at Smerwick, west of Dingle. The Irish part of the rebellion was just as ruthlessly put down: the Earl of Ormond, known as the Black Earl, killed men, women and children, took livestock and destroyed crops and houses through the length and breadth of the peninsula. As Edmund Spenser, English poet and secretary to Lord Grey, the commander of the English army, wrote: "In short space there was none almost left and a most populous and plentiful country suddenly left void of man or beast."

At the end of 1585 Queen Elizabeth announced her intention of granting Dingle a charter, setting up a town corporation, and providing for the building of a wall to enclose the commercial quarter of the town. The charter was finally granted in 1607 and provided an administrative and electoral framework for the life of the town. The corporation was governed by twelve burgesses and a sovereign, who was elected annually. The sovereign was responsible for the administration of justice, he presided over the corporation, collected customs dues and was coroner.

Dingle remained an important port and trading town in spite of the considerable destruction of the Desmond Wars, and from 1584 until the Act of Union in 1800 it returned two representatives to the Irish parliament. With the changes in the English administration of Ireland following the Act of Union, the corporation and sovereign quickly became irrelevant.

The names of the sovereigns and members of parliament are those of the Anglo-Norman ruling families of the area, in particular the Fitzgeralds. Descended from Maurice Fitzgerald, a leader of the 1169 Norman invasion of Ireland, five branches of the Geraldines held the titles, of Earl of Kildare, Earl of Desmond, Knight of Glin, Knight of Kerry and White Knight. The Knight of Kerry was based at Rahinnane in Ventry and collected rents on behalf of the Earl of Desmond. By the late sixteenth century the Fitzgeralds also held castles at Minard and Gallarus and had sold *Caisleán na bhFiach*, their castle in Dingle.

The Knight of Kerry, like most other feudal lords, attempted to safeguard his position and property after the Desmond Wars by maintaining a precarious balance between the contending forces of the English crown and those who engaged in periodic rebellions against the crown. As a result of the knight, William Fitzgerald's, failure to support the forces of Hugh O'Neill, rebel Earl of Tyrone, the Súgán Earl of Desmond burnt Dingle in 1600. In 1601 the Knight of Kerry deserted

his balancing act in favour of the Irish rebellion, and after its defeat at
the Battle of Kinsale the English army under Sir Charles Wilmot took
the castles of the knight and suppressed the rebellion in the Dingle
Peninsula. However, he was pardoned by the English, only to find himself condemned by both sides in the 1641 rebellion. In the early eighteenth century the then Knight of Kerry moved from Rahinnane to the
Grove House in Dingle.

The charter and corporation ushered in an administration of Dingle
dominated by the Fitzgeralds and other Norman families, such as the
Rices, Trants and Husseys. The wall provided for at the same time was
probably constructed over a number of years and seems also to have been
preceded by another wall. From observations of old walls and from
maps, Jack McKenna, in *Dingle . . . some of its story*, which is essential
reading for anyone wanting to know about the history of the town, gives
its route as follows:

> The wall started in the middle of Dykegate Lane. It proceeded north
> and divided what we now call the Orchard... It cut right across mod-
> ern Green St at what is now the Canon's garden. At the Presentation
> Convent grounds it turned at a right angle towards upper Main St,
> crossing the street just north of the present presbytery. At this point
> it enclosed the Knight of Kerry's castle, *Caisleán na bhFiach*, and then
> turned southwards and served as a dividing line between the Grove
> and the eastern side of Main St. This section enclosed the church of
> St James, which was situated in the old town graveyard. The final
> length of the wall cut across Main St and continued down the north-
> ern side of Dykegate Lane, thus linking up with the starting point.

Dingle suffered many years of devastation, from the Desmond Wars,
through the rebellions of 1601 and 1641 and the Cromwellian wars. A
certain amount of trade, fishing and farming continued to be carried on,
and Smith in his *History of Kerry* detailed a cargo transported from the
harbour in 1634, which included hides, butter, tallow, beef, bacon,
salmon, hake, friezes, stockings and wheat.

There was an upturn in the economy of the town in the mid-
eighteenth century with the introduction of a linen industry, which
brought considerable prosperity and employment. In 1755 an *Enquiry*

into the State and Progress of Linen Manufacture of Ireland reported that "there is not in all Munster more industrious inhabitants than on this point, between Dingle and Tralee bays". In 1756 a grant was made towards the provision of a new pier to replace the old one, known as the Spanish Pier. By the end of the century the annual sale of linen from the peninsula amounted to the extraordinarily high figure of £60,000.

A general crisis and major changes hit the textile industry in Ireland in the early nineteenth century, and Dingle's linen-based prosperity was swept away. Power spinning in cotton, and from the 1820s in linen, resulted in a dramatic shift from domestic and rural industry to factory-based industry in cities and large towns. By the 1830s the linen trade was all but gone from Dingle. The collapse came at a time when the population all over Ireland was rising rapidly – in Dingle it had reached nearly 5000 – and the decline of domestic industry was inducing chronic levels of unemployment and poverty. And it was at this time that, as a result of patterns of multiple sub-division of land, the majority of people living in the impoverished west of the country became almost exclusively dependent on the potato as a source of nourishment.

The people of Dingle and of the peninsula suffered terribly in the Famine of 1845–48. From documents of the time the inexorable progress of the tragedy can be traced. A report to Captain Hickson,

Chairman of the Dingle Relief Committee, stated, "Three-fourths of the potatoe crop, in my parish, are already spotted; and from one half to two thirds of the potatoes are totally unfit for human use." A Collector of Poor Rates wrote on 24 November 1845: "The peasantry have been actually using some of the injured potatoes, which are not fit food for even cattle let alone human beings." On 4 December Rev. James Weir, Rector of Cloghane, wrote: "One-eighth of the crop in this district is not damaged."

Famine followed famine and was followed in turn by disease. Outdoor relief schemes were brought in, but these could only benefit those fit enough to work; some indoor relief was made available, and when the Dingle workhouse could take no more other houses were opened; but the response and the resources brought to bear on the disaster were always inadequate. In common with almost everywhere in the west of Ireland, the Board of Guardians of the Dingle Union found themselves quite unable to meet the demands placed on them. The Minutes for 1 December 1849 record: "The Board having this day met solely for the purpose of investigating the claims of Paupers and after a painful day's work having filled every available accommodation in their many houses feel it quite out of their power to meet with Indoor Accommodation the frightful amount of poverty at present in the Union."

Unable to cope, the Board assisted some to emigrate. The Minutes for 5 October 1849 record the resolution "That James Sullivan be declared Contractors for supplying 40 pairs of shoes for the Emigrants at 2s 9d per pair according to pattern sent in." And the meeting of 10 October received a letter from the Poor Law Commissioners stating that: "The Ship which is to Convey the Emigrants selected from this Union is to leave Plymouth on the 22nd Instant and that it will be necessary that these parties should lie in Dublin in time for the steamer which is to leave for Plymouth on the 20th Instant."

Emigration, far from being a short-lived consequence of the Famine, became a fact of life for succeeding generations. The patterns of land holding created ingrained poverty and many tenants, unable to pay rents, were evicted in the latter part of the nineteenth century.

In the period immediately prior to the Famine, Protestants had established a vigorous mission in the Dingle Peninsula, based in Ventry. A

Catholic native of Dingle, Thomas Moriarty, became a Church of Ireland clergyman in 1838. But the impetus for the mission clearly came from England: the proselytising was led by Rev. Charles Gayer, an Englishman; funds were provided by the Irish Mission Society of London; and the missionary effort was supported by the presence of two ships of the British navy, the *Stromboli* and the *Lynx*, which were moored in Ventry and Dingle Harbours. Troops from these ships lined the streets of Dingle as Thomas Moriarty was received into the Protestant Church. The "colony" of twenty-five houses off Strand Street was established in Dingle between 1840 and 1842, and others were set up in John Street, Dingle, in Ventry, Kilmalkedar and Dunquin, all to house those who converted to Protestantism.

For a few years the mission succeeded in gaining converts, but Rev. Gayer died of famine fever in 1848 and his achievements were quickly reversed by an energetic Roman Catholic counter-offensive. The Minutes of the Board of Guardians record instances of people coming to the Board to declare publicly their reversion from Protestantism. In 1846, priests of the Vincentian order from Dublin and two Christian Brothers conducted a seven-week mission in Dingle to stem the tide of Protestantism. In 1848, the Christian Brothers established a community in Dingle, with a school in the Linen Hall in John Street. In 1851, and again in 1871, the Sisters of the Presentation Order expanded their school in Green Street. In 1862 work was begun on the present church in Green Street; in 1867 Lispole church was begun, and in 1874 Ventry church. In the grim aftermath of horrific famine, amidst conditions of continuing extreme poverty and emigration and the stirrings of Fenian rebellion and land agitation, the Roman Catholic Church established decisive allegiance and power.

After long suffering came rebellion, in the form of the Land War from 1879 to 1890 and the rise of the nationalist movement. Landlordism was assailed by physical attacks on its agents and by boycotting; evictions were carried out by the landlords, but popular solidarity held firm. Reforms in the law enabled tenants to buy their land with money loaned by the state and, parallel with the changes in proprietorship, a new middle class took over from the landed aristocracy, and in Dingle nationalists were elected to the Board of Guardians. After the Land League came the Gaelic Athletic Association, the Gaelic League and the Irish Republican Brotherhood.

Fifty years after the appalling tragedy of the Famine, an astonishing revival had taken place. The Catholic Church was at the height of its power; landlordism had been defeated and a rediscovery of the strengths in Ireland's cultural tradition, its language, literature and sports, was fuelling a broad-based political movement for independence from Britain. The Dingle Peninsula, as a repository of the Irish language and culture, became a focus for the national movement and a stronghold of the new republicanism.

The confining of the Easter Rising in 1916 almost completely to Dublin meant that Dingle played no role, though Volunteers marched into Tralee and the north coast of the peninsula was the scene of a tragic failure to land arms for the Volunteers. In the subsequent War of Independence the IRA carried out a number of relatively small-scale attacks on British forces and destroyed police barracks at Anascaul, Ballyferriter, Camp, Castlegregory and Cloghane, leaving only Dingle barracks intact. In the Civil War Dingle remained overwhelmingly republican and the Dingle barracks was then destroyed, as was the coastguard station, but towards the end of the conflict Free State troops landed at the pier and took over the town.

Peace and the Free State brought no new prosperity to Dingle and, as in other parts of the country, large numbers of young people emigrated. Significant numbers joined religious orders and many served in missions overseas. For those men who stayed behind, the football field became a prime focus of aspiration and endeavour. The area remained industrially undeveloped, its economy and employment prospects almost exclusively centred on fishing and farming.

The Irish language was given prominence in the civil service and in education in the Free State, and visitors came to the area west of Dingle to brush up on the language where it was still in everyday use. Scholars came too, from both Ireland and abroad. But the real boom in tourism was to come in the wake of the filming of *Ryan's Daughter* by David Lean in 1969. A large proportion of the massive budget for the film was spent on location in Dingle, and the direct impact of this sudden injection of money into an impoverished area, which had not yet felt the benefits of the general improvement in the Irish economy, was considerable. The exposure given to Dingle's scenery by the film was well-timed to stimulate tourism, for throughout the western world real wages were increasing, as were holidays; a "leisure market" with varying demands was growing rapidly.

Despite some diversification in employment opportunities promoted by the local authority, Údarás na Gaeltachta, the bulk of employment remains in the three categories of agriculture, fishing and tourism. In the context of the European single market, marginal regions such as west Kerry have little potential to attract manufacturing industry. While agriculture has remained important in the local economy, the policies of the EU have left many farmers dismayed and demoralised, since agriculture as they knew it clearly has no place in EU plans; as in other parts of Ireland farmers have been trying in recent years to come to terms with radically altered circumstances and to explore and develop "agri-tourism" and other alternatives. Dingle's attraction for the continental and American tourists increased in the 1970s and '80s to offset the decline in English tourists (which occurred as a consequence of the war in the North) and the presence of Fungie the dolphin brought about a boom in tourism in the late '80s which continued in the '90s. Since the 1994 IRA cessation there has been a marked increase in British visitors, many of whom are keen to explore the joys of rambling.

Fishing has suffered from lack of government and EU policies to exploit its potential, but a substantial development of the harbour between 1989 and 1992 resulted in a dramatic increase in the number and tonnage of boats fishing out of Dingle. This increased employment both on boats and on shore. However, the fleet is ageing, prices for catches are low, and many other problems make of the fishing industry a lost opportunity for this western port of an island nation. Increased tourism has benefited proprietors of tourist-related businesses, but a large proportion of the jobs in the restaurants and hotels are only seasonal, summer jobs. The pattern remains of the young people of Dingle aspiring to pursue careers far from their home town, in Ireland, Europe and the United States, but there has been a real improvement in the range of jobs available to young people.

Dingle enjoyed new prosperity in the 1990s, and it shows. New supermarkets, farm mart, renovated public houses, freshly painted private houses and an enormously increased number of guesthouses all testify to a level of activity and available income which compares well with other communities in Ireland. While the permanent population of the town has declined to its present level of about 1400, the sons and daughters of the place who work and study elsewhere return regularly and frequently, expressing an identification and satisfaction with the resources of their home town. For a community of its size, it possesses facilities – partly on account of the tourist industry – which few communities twice its size can boast.

There is a vibrancy about life in the town, and social and material modernisation has gone hand-in-hand with renewed enthusiasm for traditions such as the Wren's Day and the Blessing of the Boats, for traditional Irish music and set-dancing. Irish people – indeed, the Celts in general – have been renowned for centuries for their enjoyment of festive occasions. The hilltop assemblies of Lughnasa and the celebrations at holy wells are no more, but the peninsula's *naomhóg* regattas provide festivals in summer, and the Dingle Races in August make for a colourful long weekend. Other occasions such as the West Kerry Agricultural Show add to the festive calendar and contribute to a sense of almost continuous festival during the summer months.

But the most important festival, organised by and for the local community, is the "Wren's Day", which takes place on St Stephen's Day, 26 December every year, come rain, hail or snow. Not an occasion for the visitor, it is nevertheless a vital local custom of a kind which was once practised throughout Europe. I have described it in a book – *Green and Gold: the Wrenboys of Dingle* – but its main appearance is of a parade of people dressed in straw suits and other costumes, preceded by hobby horse and banner and accompanied by the marching music of fife and drum and other bands. For many people who have emigrated from Dingle over the years, the "Wren's Day" is the day when their thoughts are most likely to dwell on their home town.

Beatha an Scoláire

Leagtha ar Chearbhall Ó Dálaigh, fl 1597-1630
ar fáil uainn sa chnuasach Nua-Dhuanaire I

Aoibhinn beatha an scoláire
bhíos ag déanamh a léighinn;
is follas díbh, a dhaoine,
gurab dó is aoibhne in Éirinn.

Gan smacht ríogh ná rófhlatha
ná tighearna dá threise,
gan chuid cíosa ag caibidil,
gan moichéirghe, gan meirse.

Moichéirghe ná aodhaireacht
ní thabhair uadha choidhche,
's ní mó do-bheir dá aire
fear na faire san oidhche.

Maith biseach a sheisrighe
ag teacht tosaigh an earraigh;
is é is crannghail dá sheisrigh
lán a ghlaice de pheannaibh.

Do-bheir sé greas ar tháiplis,
is ar chláirsigh go mbinne,
nó fós greas eile ar shuirghe
is ar chumann mná finne.

An Café Liteartha
Bóthar an Dadhgaide, An Daingean.
www.cafelit.com; soluasa@cafelit.com.

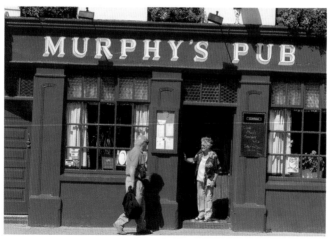

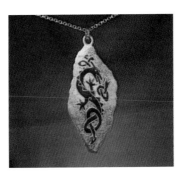

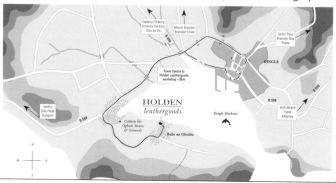

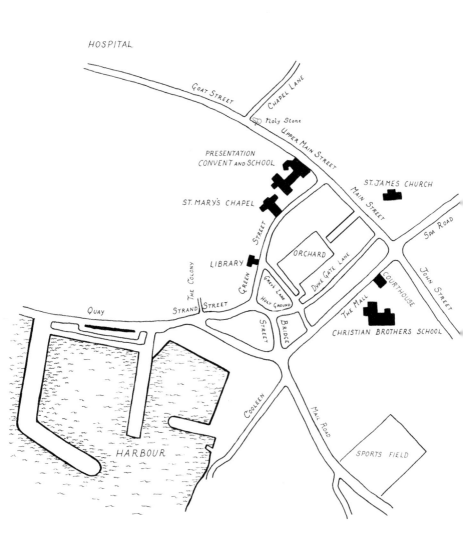

The Streets of Dingle

MAIN STREET HAS always been the commercial sector of the town. Today it contains the two banks, the credit union, about ten pubs, several restaurants and a variety of shops, including the largest hardware shop.

The Church of Ireland church on the north side of Main Street, St James's, was built in 1807 and renovated in 1974; an earlier church on the same site was reputed to have been built by the Spaniards. Its dedication to St James and the Spanish trading presence in the town lends support to the tradition; Dingle was also a point of embarkation for the popular medieval pilgrimage to the shrine of St James at Compostella. In a side chapel is a broken memorial to John Fitzgerald, Knight of Kerry, who died in 1741. Near by, in what remains of the old Dingle graveyard, is a curious slab from a tomb; broken now, the inscription around the edge of the slab is no longer legible, but it recorded, in an abbreviated form of mixed Latin and Irish, the burial of one of the Fitzgeralds in 1504.

Above the credit union stands the Temperance Hall and opposite it a building which was until recent years the presbytery. Here, in 1792, in what was then the house of James Louis Rice, Count of the Holy Roman Empire, it is said that rooms were prepared for Marie Antoinette. Son of a shipper of wines from Ballymacadoyle in Dingle, James Rice became a senior officer in the Austrian army and a close friend of the Emperor of Austria. Marie Antoinette was a sister of the emperor and it seems that a group of officers of the Irish Brigade, led by Rice, planned to rescue her

from imprisonment in the Temple in Paris and bring her to Dingle on one of the family wine ships. However, the queen apparently proved unwilling to abandon her husband and children, and the plan came to nothing.

In **Upper Main Street** stands the convent of the Presentation order, founded in 1829. The present building dates in the main to 1878, though an extra wing was added in 1892. It now houses the primary school for girls and boys and the secondary school for girls. Numbers attending the schools in early 2000 were 311. The rest of the convent is now home to the Díseart Celtic Educational and Cultural Institute, continuing the religious tradition of the building, which includes a beautiful chapel featuring Spanish oak stalls and twelve outstanding stained glass windows by Harry Clarke.

Further up the street and on the opposite side, a large boulder, or *bullán*, lies near the corner of Chapel Lane. Known as the Holy (or, more correctly, Holey) Stone, it has several cup-shaped pits, a form of decoration most commonly associated with the Bronze Age. Tradition has it that such stones played a role in pagan worship and more recent folklore maintains that the holes were used for holding holy water. It is an important landmark and reference point in Dingle, featuring in several local songs.

Chapel Lane takes its name from the Roman Catholic church that stood there through the eighteenth century. The family and musical traditions of Chapel Lane combined with those of neighbouring Goat Street and Upper Main Street to make this a lively part of town until it gradually became depopulated through emigration, so that in recent decades comparative silence has settled on it.

There are houses now on only one side of **Goat Street**, but the wall on the other side is a series of what were once the fronts of houses, their windows and doors now blocked up. There was a Fair Field here, which featured in the bitter divisions associated with the fall of Parnell, the great political leader of the 1870s and 1880s. An author who was close to the events of that time, Patrick Foley, wrote in his *History of the County Kerry: Corkaguiney* (1907):

> When the Irish National Land League was started in Dingle, the cattle and pig fairs were removed by the leaguers to Goat Street, and a

Registered Patent taken out, which instrument was never used for weighing cattle more than twice. When this unfortunate split took place, the anti-Parnellite priests headed their followers in a combination for the destruction of the Parnellite leaders in the town, with the result that the cattle fair was carried to the Spa Road, while the Parnellite pig buyers succeeded in keeping the pig fair in Goat Street.

At the same time Dingle boasted a fine brass and reed band, but as its members would not renounce Parnell, this band was broken up by the clergy. In such seemingly small yet socially vital ways a traumatic political split was reflected in towns throughout Ireland.

Above Goat Street, on the slope of *Cnoc an Chairn*, stands Dingle hospital, site of an earlier workhouse, and beyond it stands a row of cottages at Ashmount. To the north of the hospital is the old graveyard of *Cill Mhairéad*, where those who died in the workhouse were buried. In four years of the Famine some 6000 people passed through Dingle workhouse, many dying there and being buried here on the hillside. As is clear from the Minutes of the Poor Law Guardians, so overwhelming was the task of attempting to provide relief that records could not be adequately kept, and local historians can only guess at the numbers who died and were buried at *Cill Mhairéad* on the slopes of *Cnoc an Chairn*. In 1986, as part of a festival to celebrate aspects of local heritage and culture, this sad, overgrown graveyard was tidied up and a religious service was held on the site. Those who had died and been buried had done so without the assistance or presence of clergy, and now, at last, they were given some form of posthumous recognition, their place in Dingle's history acknowledged.

Green Street is dominated by St Mary's Roman Catholic church. Completed in 1865, it replaced a church built on the same site in 1812. It is a fine building, expressing well the new confidence of Catholicism in Dingle at that time, and is built of stone quarried at Kilmurry and brought by boat to Dingle. A memorial tablet in a side walls records that:

Underneath lie the remains of Clarissa Hussey who died August 14th, 1864, aged over 80 years. During life she had been a most bountiful benefactress to the religious and charitable institutions of her native town, and for the same purpose she bequeathed all her property. This church has been erected chiefly at her expense. As it is her resting-place so let it be her monument. People of Dingle pray for her soul.

She was a sister of Sam Hussey, an infamous landlord's agent, and a note in Patrick Foley's *History* (1907) suggests that her evident generosity to the church was not matched by a similar generosity to her tenants: "There is no doubt," he wrote, "but this landlady ranked amongst the worst landowners in the country."

Near the corner of Green Street with Main Street, a stone inscribed with the date 1586 is set into the upper-storey wall of a fish-and-chip shop. It undoubtedly came from one of the many houses built after the destruction of the town in the Desmond Wars. Further down the street other houses boast small decorated panels which are said to have came from the houses of Spanish merchants in the town; tradition has it that they indicated the nature of the business carried on.

The public library has a display of material relating to the Irish patriot Thomas Ashe and an interesting collection of books donated by the writer Padraig Ó Siochfradha (*An Seabhac*). The large house on the opposite side of the road, now a solicitor's office and home, was previously the residence of Captain de Moleyns, a brother of Lord Ventry.

In **Gray's Lane** is the entrance to the Orchard, which is sometimes more correctly referred to as the Archard Field, for its name comes from the practice of archery here. A public park with tennis courts, its far wall, which runs parallel with Main Street, follows the route of the old town walls.

Dykegate Lane derives its name from the time when the town was walled, for it is *Bóthar an Dhá Geata*, the street of the two gates. There was a gallows here, too. Now there is a bookshop/café, a wholefood shop, a craft shop, two bicycle hire businesses and a comfortable cinema and video store. For a town its size Dingle was perhaps lucky in having a cinema from the 1920s, and it was for many decades the place for dances. Active clerical disapproval of dances went to the extent of a priest parading in front of the cinema with a placard reading, on the front – "You go in a lady," and on the back – "You come out a ?" Some people may have been intimidated, but others merely used the side entrance!

In **The Mall**, beside which runs the Dingle River, St John's holy well was once regularly visited. Beside O'Connor's garage is a monument to those who died in the fight for independence. There was a Protestant school in the Mall, which was used for editing during the filming of *Ryan's Daughter*.

Behind the courthouse stands the monastery and school of the Christian Brothers, which was built in 1873. Numbers attending the school in early 1993 were 250. The Brothers came to Dingle in 1848 and opened their first school in the Linen Hall in **John Street**, which had fallen into disuse with the decline of the linen industry. On the site of the Christian Brothers' school once stood an army barracks, built in 1702, and the part of John Street near it is still known as the Barrack Height. In the lane from John Street to the monastery was a popular dancing platform known as the "Quarter Deck".

Populated in the nineteenth century primarily by weavers and nail makers, John Street was the main road into Dingle from the east until the Mail Road was brought around on the present main route via Ballintaggart. Galvin's has a long history as a travel agency, and for thousands of emigrants represented the first step on a long and traumatic journey to a new life. Every street has its own distinctive character, and John Street is the one that seems closest to the surrounding countryside, its preoccupations and activities having mostly to do with farming.

Many visitors enter Dingle by the road that leads over the mountains by the Connor Pass; this brings them in past the creamery and the

Hillgrove Hotel and the **Spa Road**. Only a few decades ago a line of ponies and traps would stretch along the road from the creamery, and farmers would exchange news as they waited to deliver their milk. The name of the road comes from an impregnated well in the townland of Ballybeg. At the time of the linen industry the Bleach Green was beside the Spa Road, and the most substantial business done here now is at the Mart, which was once the site of a brewery. To the right as one enters the town is the Grove, now a housing estate, where the house of the Knight of Kerry once stood.

At the seaward end of the Mall is Hudson's Bridge, near which **Cooleen** extends along the water's edge. It was to here that many families of fishermen were moved when Lord Ventry cleared the Burnham Peninsula, including what was then the fishing village of Reenbeg. The second-last house on the right, now a natural healing centre, was a coast-guards' watchhouse.

The Garda barracks (or police station) stands in **Bridge Street** on the site of an earlier barracks burnt down in the Civil War. Opposite it, O'Flaherty's is a favourite venue for tourists who like to hear Irish music while comparing notes with fellow-travellers and imbibing the ambience along with pints of "the black stuff". Irish traditional music is, by its nature, generally informal, and those who demand set times and days will find that, although there is music here almost every night in the summer, the best music often happens in impromptu sessions. Some of the musicians who play in Dingle pubs and hotels are from the Dingle area, but many have settled here, attracted both by the charms of the place and by the fact that musicians are in demand and much appreciated. There is an atmosphere and a lively informality about the pubs of Dingle that appeals to many visitors from all over the world, as well as from Ireland. In recent years the traditional "session", which gives so much to the character of Irish music in practice, has been largely replaced in Dingle by amplified performances, and a great deal of the music itself has changed to accommodate a rock beat. Sessions are generally to be found in less touristed parts of the peninsula, and of Ireland generally, but are more difficult to locate since they are less advertised.

Like the Holy Stone, there is nothing holy about **Holy Ground**; the name comes from the holes left in the ground by tanneries that

previously existed here. Outside the Forge restaurant stands a relic of the old forge – a ship's spar used for bending metal. In Greany's restaurant is an excellent photograph of the old smith at work.

Busy now with shops and pubs, **Strand Street** scarcely existed until the late nineteenth century, apart from a few fishermen's cabins. A group of houses above it is the Quay Colony, built by the Protestant missionaries; where it meets Strand Street is still called the "Colony Gate". An entrance above the pier is known as the Clyde Gate, after the Clyde Shipping Company, which once did business here. Beside the head of the pier is the boatyard, now closed down. The decline in the fishing industry in recent years has been marked by the emigration of many Dingle fishermen and boatyard workers.

The pier and harbour are the scene in August of one of Dingle's annual festivals, the regatta. Smaller regattas take place around the peninsula – at Ballydavid, Brandon and Maharees – and all these regattas feature the distinctive black canvas-covered boat known as the *naomhóg* (pronounced "nayvogue"), which is rowed with bladeless oars. At the turn of the century many hundreds of these craft – also called canoes and, elsewhere in Ireland, curraghs – were in daily use for fishing. In its traditional design the Dingle Peninsula canoe possesses an outstanding, simple elegance, particularly in the ascending curve of its raised prow. Exceptionally light and manoeuvrable, the traditional canoe, with its high gunwhale and prow, tends to be caught by the wind, and so the racing canoe which is now built and used is a cut-down and less elegant craft. Since the harbour redevelopment of 1989–92 the Dingle Regatta has, unfortunately, lost its physical focus. Land reclaimed from the sea has been made into a carpark, sadly destroying the intimate relationship between this part of the town and the sea, a relationship which was essential to the particular attractiveness of Dingle as a town.

To the west of the pier a line of houses built in 1909 and known as "the cottages", extends along the harbour's edge in the townland of *An Choill* (The Wood) towards Milltown. There is no sign now of the wood, nor of the 56 houses which stood here in 1852.

GREENLANE GALLERY DINGLE

Co. Kerry, Ireland

Tel: 066 9152018 / 9152199   Fax: 066 9151202   Mobile: 086 8044757
email: info@GreenlaneGallery.com
web: www.GreenlaneGallery.com

Contemporary painting and sculpture by leading Irish artists.

ACCOMMODATION   Our accommodation consists of self-catering apartments available for weekly rental. These are adjacent to Dingle Horse Riding facilities and offer access to spectacular hill walking routes. Please see our apartment web pages for more information.

www.DingleHorseRiding.com

Dingle horse riding

Dingle Horse Riding is Irish Tourist Board approved and a member of A.I.R.E. (The Association of Irish Riding Establishments).

James Thompson & Susan Callery
Ballinaboula, Dingle,
Co. Kerry, Ireland

Tel   +353 66 9152018
      +353 66 9152199
Fax +353 66 9151202
Mobile   086 8137917

email: info@DingleHorseRiding.com
website: www.DingleHorseRiding.com

near by and a *gallán* was erected, and in the years that followed her funeral games were celebrated.

Different versions of the story of the battle exist in medieval manuscripts. They present a confused and evidently non-historical picture but, significantly, they show a close familiarity with local topography. It is probably the case that elements of disparate tales of Fionn Mac Cúmhaill and the Fianna were grafted on to the setting of the harbour of Ventry and its surrounds. As Eugene O'Curry wrote, in *Manuscript Materials of Ancient Irish History*, the *Cath Finntrágha*, or "Battle of Ventry", is "of no absolute value as historic authority for the incidents related in it; but the many names of places, and the various manners and customs traditionally handed down and preserved in it, render it of considerable interest to the student of Irish history".

Placenames which reflect the violent events of the battle survive in the area. There are fields called *Cluain na Fola* – field of blood – and *Cúin na dtréan Fhir* – slaughter of mighty men. At Parkmore Point in Cuan is *Rinn na Bairce* – barque point – to which the traitor Glas piloted the invaders. The bogland at the border of the townlands of Caheratrant and Raheen was once an oak forest where the Fianna engaged in their favourite occupation, hunting.

THE HILL immediately behind Ventry, to the north, is Caherard. Taking the road uphill from Quinn's pub and past the post office, bear left at the top around the foot of the hill and continue to a disused quarry. Inside the gate on the left is a track and from here it is a short walk up to the summit where there is a megalithic wedge grave known as *Leaba an Fhir Mhúimhnuigh*, the Munsterman's Bed. It is of the same kind and period as the graves at Maumnahaltora. This can be a short excursion, or the start of a long walk.

To the north of the grave the hill dips down to a saddle where the old road, Bóthar a' Cínn, crosses the hill. This is the road on which Peig Sayers and others from the Blasket Islands and Dunquin travelled to Dingle and it is now part of the Dingle Way. If returning to the quarry, one can follow the surfaced road back around the foot of the hill, taking a left turn up to Caherboshina – *Cathair Bó Sine*, variously translated as the stone fort of the old cow, the cow's teat, Sínch's hut, or the rainbow. North of Caherboshina is Ballymorereagh (locals drop the "more"). On the slopes of the hill above are the oratory and grave of St Manchan. A settlement of about the seventh to ninth centuries, it never developed into a later church site. It is a relatively well preserved oratory, known as both *Teampall Mhanachain* and *Teampall Geal* – the white (or bright) church, and it is very similar in design and construction to Gallarus oratory. One of the cross-slabs of this early Christian site has both ogham and Latin inscriptions.

At a well near by a very popular "pattern" used to be held on Easter Sunday, at which a fiddler from Dingle played at the crossroads. Such entertainments came under attack from the clergy from quite early in the nineteenth century; priests were not above smashing musical instruments and preventing traditional musicians from earning any kind of living. Breandán Breathnach, in *Dancing in Ireland* (Dal gCais, 1983), writes of Fr John Casey, nineteenth-century parish priest of Ballyferriter, that he was "a deadly enemy of pipers and cardplayers. He stopped the music, dancing and card playing in his parish and Tom Kennedy, the old blind piper who gave Canon Goodman several hundred tunes, turned Protestant and joined the souper colony at Ventry." He also quotes from an account by Fr O'Sullivan of Dingle of an occasion when Fr Casey found music being played: "He rushed over, laid hold of the innocent if unfortunate piper, kicked, cuffed and beat him unmercifully, broke his

pipes and completely dispersed the whole assembly." Fr Casey was by no means alone and had a century of successors around the peninsula and, indeed, around Ireland. While some wells are still visited for the purpose of devotions and cures, the "patterns" as entertainments were finally stamped out in the peninsula by about 1940.

From St Manchan's the walker can strike uphill to the ridge and take in the view to the west while pursuing the line of the ridge. Descending at Maumanorig, near Caherard there is a cluster of houses. Below the road, about two hundred yards from the bend in the road, is Kilcolman, the remains of an early Christian settlement. The roughly circular enclosure of about 148 feet (45 metres) in diameter includes within it the foundations of huts, several graves and gravestones, a cross-inscribed ogham stone, a small cross-inscribed stone, a holed stone and three bullauns. Below this early Christian settlement lies St Brendan's holy well, and above it in the field fence bordering on the bohareen is another cross-slab. The most notable element of the site is its ogham-inscribed cross-slab, which stands in the south-east corner of the site. The ogham inscription runs up the left-hand side and over the top of the main cross; although very legible, the inscription has puzzled archaeologists, but it is thought it is meant to read: ANM COLMAN AILITHIR – "Colman the Pilgrim".

The bohareen continues towards a junction beside the dramatic ruins of

Rahinnane Castle. This is a splendid example of a large ringfort having been reused at a later date. Believed to have been the rath of the prominent local family of early times, the O'Falveys, it has a high rampart and deep ditch, and in the southern sector of the ditch a souterrain opens at the base of the rampart. Approximately 131 feet (40 metres) in diameter, the rath has double banks and a wide fosse which is up to 26 feet (8 metres) deep in parts. The souterrain is blocked up now, but the nineteenth-century archaeologist Hitchcock described entering it in 1854 and finding an extensive underground complex of passages tunnelled out of the earth.

The ruined castle was the principal tower-house of the Knights of Kerry; several similar castles were built in the sixteenth century, some at least with the help of a £10 grant from the English government. It was captured by Sir Charles Wilmot in 1602 and was later "slighted" by the Cromwellian forces.

The fort and castle command a magnificent view of Ventry Harbour and the surrounding countryside, and it is easy to see why the site was chosen. Strangely susceptible to changes in light, sometimes the castle stands out strongly and the ramparts are barely visible; sometimes it is the ringfort that seizes one's attention. It possesses a powerful atmosphere, perhaps partly owing to the shape of the hills behind; and it is a place to think of on *Samhain* eve – Hallowe'en – when the fairies were said to emerge from the forts and roam the countryside.

It was popularly believed about many such castles that the strength of the mortar in them was due to the mixing in it of blood. And here at Rahinnane it was said to have been the blood of local people. It seems that the centuries have carried down some residue of feudal cruelty. Local historian Doncha Ó Conchúir has suggested in his book *Corca Dhuibhne* that the population of the settlement of beehive huts at Fahan, some five or six miles to the south-west, might have been labourers or serfs who worked the fertile land of Ventry for the ruling O'Falvey family well before the advent of the Anglo-Norman rulers.

The bohareen from Kilcolman used to continue past the farm buildings at Rahinnane and rise gently along the foot of the hill to the pass known as the *Mám Clasach* and the road to Dunquin. This, again, was the route on which the people of the Blaskets travelled to Dingle. It is still clearly defined and walk-able in parts and visitors with sturdy boots and thorn-proof clothes might enjoy exploring it. It was not, unfortunately, possible to include it in the Dingle Way because of the difficulty of maintaining it in a passable condition.

KILDURRIHY (*Cill idir dá shruth*, the church between two streams) is the site of a *ceallúnach* or burial ground and of Templebeg, a small church of which very little remains and which was probably of the eighth or ninth century. The cluster of houses that make up Kildurrihy is a fine example of what is meant by a "clachan". The word, from the Scots Gaelic, is used to describe communities which are smaller than villages and somewhat different in terms of social organisation, reflecting the patterns of land holding and use. It was long the characteristic unit of life on the peninsula, but in recent years it has been abandoned in favour of houses scattered singly.

Beside the road in Kildurrihy is a *bullán*, a very large boulder with a series of rounded depressions on its surface. It is similar to the Holy Stone in Dingle and St Brendan's Keelers in Kilmalkedar. These boulders might have served for community corn-grinding, but the depressions seem too small and inconveniently placed. The stones could perhaps have held in their cups material associated with pre-Christian religion – herbal preparations or oils. Elsewhere in Ireland *bulláin* were used in living memory for making ground bait for limpets; and some which had small stones within the cups were regarded as "cursing stones": the stones would be turned three times in the opposite direction to the movement of the sun to effect the curse. The fact that most *bullán* are found near or at ancient religious sites supports the notion that they were associated with rituals of some sort. E. Estyn Evans, in *Irish Folk Ways*, expresses "little doubt that they were the communal mortars of pre-Christian settlements".

A holy well at the northern side of Kildurrihy is dedicated to St Brendan, on whose feast-day it used to be visited. Beside the well lies a shaped stone, broken in half, a sort of tablet, which is said to have been stolen away once but to have made its own way back. In recent years a modern stone has also been placed in the well. The Pilgrim's Route continues north along a track from St Brendan's Well towards Coumaleague, where it crosses a stream before reaching the *Mám Clasach* road. On the slopes of Coumaleague Hill one can easily make out, especially in evening light, the parallel lines of old cultivation ridges.

In many such places on the slopes of hills old ridges of tillage like these can be seen, even up to heights of 2000 feet. In some cases these reflect a time of higher population when a greater acreage was tilled; in other cases they tell a story of starving people seeking out isolated, poor land from which to scrape some kind of existence after famine and eviction. But mostly they were places of summer tillage, known as *crích*, which in English is a corn-ridge. Such tillage, with soil piled in ridged beds, went on side-by-side with booleying (also termed transhumance) whereby cattle were taken to mountain pastures in the summer. Many of the *clochán* in the hills were built in relatively recent history to house the young people who tended the livestock and to store butter and cheese.

There is a saying about the corn-ridges which is current here as in some other parts of the country:

> Trí each marcach,
> Trí marcach fiolar,
> Trí fiolar iúr,
> Trí iúr crích,
> Trí chrí deireadh an domhain.

The extraordinary economy of the statement in Irish is impossible to reproduce in English, but a rough translation would be:

Three life-spans of a horse: a man,
Three life-spans of a man: an eagle,
Three life-spans of an eagle: a yew-tree,
Three life-spans of a yew-tree: a corn-ridge,
Three life-spans of a corn-ridge: the end of the world.

From Kildurrihy a stony road rises to Mount Eagle Lake, a delightful place to fish or just to walk or sit. In evening light the steep cliff to the mountain summit looms magnificently. Beside the lake is a zig-zag turf track which provides a walk with excellent views on a fine day; and from the summit there is another track down to the Dunquin road. A great day's walking can be had by setting out from Ventry, taking in some or all of the sites such as Caherard, Kilcolman, Rahinnane and Kildurrihy, climbing Mount Eagle and dropping down then into Dunquin for a well-earned drink at Kruger's, and returning to Ventry via Slea Head, Fahan and Kilvickadownig. A long walk, but a memorable one through scenery the equal of which can rarely be found.

The next cluster of houses after Kildurrihy is Ballintlea. Where the road crosses a stream the townland of Kildurrihy East yields to Ballintlea and a track rises to the right and continues uphill beside the stream. Indeed, for a short distance the stream takes over in wet weather and a pathway runs beside it. Passing stone houses, the bohareen swings left

just below Caherlea, a stone fort containing a particularly interesting souterrain complex. The caher is about ninety feet in diameter, with thick enclosure walls a few feet high. The ground level within it has risen considerably, and stones exposed amidst the growth of grass, bracken and brambles are likely to be the remains of beehive huts. In the wall at the southern side of the caher is a ruined *clochán*, most of which now lies below the level of the earth and rubble inside the enclosure. From the base of the *clochán* four low exits lead off, apparently to underground chambers at least one of which appears to be within the caher wall.

The next townland gets its name from a caher that has disappeared. But the main point of interest about the name of Caherbullig is that it records the name of Bolg, the principal god of the *Fir Bolg*, the pre-Celtic people who are thought to have settled here. Bolg, like most of the gods, had alternate names and personas, one of which was Daire, who took the form of the King of the World, Daire Donn, in the battle of Ventry. The name of the townland south of Caherbullig, Kilvickadownig, probably derives from the association with Daire Donn, who is buried here.

Beside the road at Kilvickadownig, near a bend, stands a small schoolhouse; close by, a bohareen leads up off the road. A short distance along the bohareen is a farmhouse with a gate beside it; behind the house is a *gallán*, or standing stone, known as "The Stone of the Moon". In the middle of the next field up is *Leac a' Ré*, a stone said to commemorate the King of the World. It is marked with an interesting Greek cross enclosed within a sweeping design of elegant simplicity. A short distance from the stone is the site of an early Christian settlement with a fine pillar-stone inscribed with crosses on two sides. This may have been a pre-Christian site which was taken over by the early Christians, though there is no evidence of a chamber tomb referred to in some reports. In fields near by and beside the bohareen, a little to the north, are the remains of several *clochán*, some of which are in very good condition.

From the schoolhouse the road continues towards the coastline, and in a field on the right stands a ringfort, clearly visible from the road. Inside the enclosure are the remains of various stone structures, including part of an exposed souterrain.

Páidí O Sé's pub - Ventry, Ireland.
Tel: 066 9159011

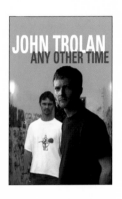

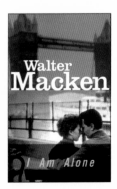

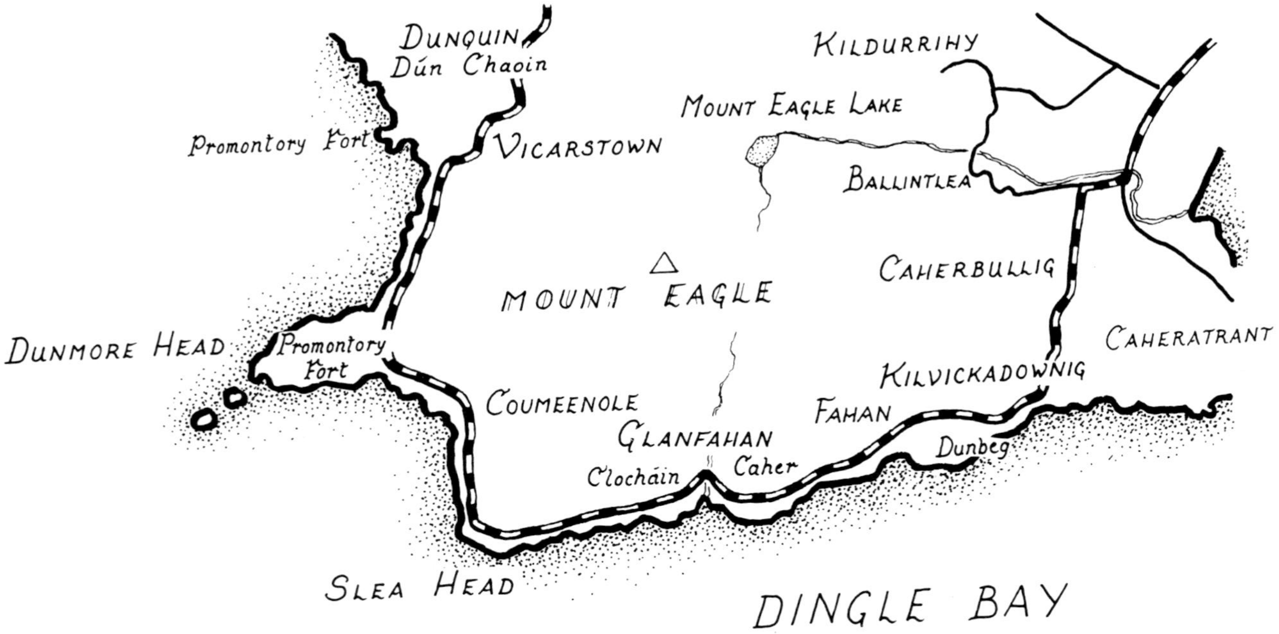

DINGLE BAY

Caheratrant

Kildurrihy

Mount Eagle Lake

Ballintlea

Caherbullig

Kilvickadownig

Dunbeg

Fahan

Mount Eagle

Glanfahan

Coumeenole

Caher

Clocháin

Vicarstown

Dunquin
Dún Chaoin

Promontory Fort

Promontory Fort

Dunmore Head

Slea Head

Fahan

I N KILVICKADOWNIG AN old track crosses the road and the crossroads is marked by a boulder. The track leading west is part of the Dingle Way and is excellently suited to the rambler, as it allows for exploring an area of breathtaking coastal scenery and of great archaeological interest away from the noise and fumes of traffic on the road. Running parallel with the surfaced road and above it, this track offers a better view from its higher vantage point, with the remains of beehive huts above and below for most of the way as far as Coumeenole. But by car one should continue on the road as it swings right along the coast.

Below the track, and above the road, where some Ordnance Survey maps indicate a cross, an unusual small stone cross lies atop a small mound of loose stones which are partially covered by grass. One of very few early stone crosses, as opposed to cross-slabs, it lies about twenty-five yards from the remains of a stone-walled enclosure. Both cross and enclosure are of the early Christian period.

So many are the archaeological remains in this narrow strip of coastline at the foot of the hills that it would require a whole book to describe them all. Shortly I shall describe in some detail the promontory fort of Dunbeg, but apart from that I shall just indicate briefly some of the sites along our route. Any visitor interested in looking more deeply into the archaeology of this fascinating area of Fahan should go to a library and study R.A.S. Macalister's extensive work, *On an ancient settlement in the south-west of the Barony of Corkaguiney, Kerry* (Transactions of the Royal Irish Academy 31, 1899).

The old track dips down to the cluster of houses at Fahan, where a bohareen from the main road below meets it. Beyond some ruined houses one track continues straight ahead for a short distance and another turns right. There is a house on the corner here, and opposite it, just below and beside the track, is what looks like an old shed and nothing more. However, it is attached to the ruins of a small early Christian church, known as *Teampall Beag*, on top of which lies a cross-slab.

The walk along the old road continues on the track that swings right uphill at the house. But walkers should detour to visit *Dún Beag* promontory fort, taking the bohareen down to the main road.

People travelling by car or bike from Kilvickadownig will see signposts and a carpark for Dunbeg, or *Dún Beag* (the small fort), which is one of the most elaborate promontory forts in Ireland. Iron Age in type, recent excavation has shown that it continued to be occupied at intervals at least until the late medieval period. Rarely, if ever, a place of prolonged habitation, it probably served as some kind of refuge at times of danger.

The promontory is defended by five lines of fosses, four lines of banks and a dry-stone rampart. Despite the fact that erosion of the cliffs has robbed the rampart of half its length, it is still impressive, standing up to 10 feet (3 metres) high and up to 21 feet (6 metres) thick, with three inner ledges or terraces. On either side of the entrance there are small chambers inside the rampart, and the entrance itself features holes in which a wooden bar could be inserted to support a door.

At some stage in its existence the rampart was reinforced. The exterior capstone of the entrance roof of the earlier wall is cracked, and this probably gave rise to the later part of the wall being built to provide support.

The approach to the rampart entrance must once have been impressive; a causeway through the fosses is flanked by orthostats – upright stones – at the two banks closest to the rampart and probably originally at the other banks also. Beneath the causeway a souterrain runs from just inside the entrance as far as the second bank from the rampart. It is 54 feet (16.5 metres) long and was built of dry-stone walls roofed with large slabs; at the outer end there is a semicircular well and what may have been a ventilation shaft.

Within the enclosure made by the rampart is a large *clochán* which is circular on the outside and rectangular on the inside (a characteristic also of smaller *clochán* in the monastery of Skellig Michael). On the inside of the entrance are stone supports for a door and there are holes for a wooden bar. It is very unlikely that the roof of the *clochán* was ever of stone; instead, wood and wattle structures were erected inside it.

Few of the many coastal promontory forts have been excavated; and what excavations have taken place have yielded little evidence; but in general such sites are dated from the Iron Age or Early Christian period. Dunbeg was excavated in 1977 by T.B. Barry, who concluded in his report that, "The series of radiocarbon dates at Dunbeg together with its structural parallels to other European stone forts would point to either an Iron Age or Early Christian date for its construction."

Evidence of two distinct occupation layers was found in the *clochán*, both belonging to the tenth or eleventh centuries. Nothing was found to suggest a date for the souterrain. The fosse closest to the rampart produced evidence that it was in use in the eighth or ninth century, but no finds yielded dates for the rampart or for the lapse of time between its first and supplementary stages.

Beneath the rampart, however, a shallow ditch ran for some 19 metres from inside the line of the later entrance towards the south-east. Some stones were found along the bottom of the ditch and these could have come from an early dry-stone wall. Also, there was a layer of charcoal along the whole length of this ditch which probably derived from wattle fencing. This charcoal layer yielded a radiocarbon date of 580 BC and thus a ditch, dry-stone wall and wattle fence probably represent the first stage of human occupation of the promontory.

The rampart, fosses and banks constituted substantial defences. The souterrain, too, was probably defensive – a hiding place in time of attack, or possibly even a means of surprising attackers from behind. But the reasons for creating such elaborate defences on a rocky promontory remain far from clear. It is, of course, possible to speculate and many people have, suggesting that such forts were the last bolt-holes of a people in retreat from Iron Age invaders. It has also been suggested – and this seems more likely – that they were the first fortified footholds of the invaders, from which they advanced to control the area. Certainly Dunbeg and many similar sites seem to have been occupied only briefly, if on more than one occasion. As Barry comments, "The lack of any occupation debris calls into question the motives of the people who built such complex defensive sites and then never seemed to occupy them for any appreciable length of time."

Almost every defensible promontory on the west coast of Ireland was defended with various arrangements of banks, fosses or stone walls. Similar forts are common along the coasts of Devon, Cornwall and Somerset in England, in Wales, Scotland, the Isle of Man and Brittany. There are particular similarities between Dunbeg and forts in Scotland – at the Ness of Burgi and at Nybster in Caithness. And similar terracing is found at Portadoona and Carrigillihy in west Cork, Staigue in Kerry, the Grianán of Aileach in Donegal, Gurnard's Head in Cornwall and Kercaradec in Brittany. From what little evidence has emerged from the excavations of promontory forts, a link is suggested with the Venetic area of Brittany. It may be that future excavations will support the notion that they constitute the bridgeheads of colonisation by the Veneti in the Iron Age.

What remains of Dunbeg is impressive in construction and it is enhanced by its position on the rocky cliffs of the southern coastline of the peninsula. Where invaders of the Iron Age may have set up their defences, seals now bask in the sea below and many distinctive birds skirt the cliffs and wheel overhead. This is an area particularly frequented by seabirds such as gannets and fulmars, but once it was famous for hawks, especially the peregrine falcons which were exported for the sport of European nobility from the medieval period. The fulmars came here only at the turn of the century, adopting the area as a dispersal point; and their magnificent gliding may be seen along the coast from Kilvickadownig to Dunquin and on the Blasket Islands.

The gannets to be seen here come from the Little Skellig Island to the south, which is the second largest gannetry in the world, with about 25,000 pairs. They may be seen diving from heights of about fifty feet, easily distinguishable by their yellow beaks and black-tipped wings from the other divers encountered along this coast, the great northern diver and the terns. Another bird encountered on the cliffs near Dunbeg is the chough, which can provide an experience which is at once startling and exhilarating, as it has a habit of flying very close as one stands on the cliffs. With bright red bill and red legs it nests here on the cliffs and flies up to the mountains to feed.

On the land to the east of Dunbeg the fields in autumn are covered with the yellow-flowering *buachaillán buí* or ragwort, and almost every inch of these plants is in turn covered with brown and yellow-striped caterpillars of the cinnabar moth, a black-and-red moth which flies by day.

A few fields east of Dunbeg, fifty yards from the road, are the remains of an enclosure, featuring part of a stone wall characteristic of early Christian sites and low earthen bank continuing the circle of the wall. The butt of an axehead dating from about 3000 BC was found here in 1981, indicating that this area was inhabited in neolithic times.

Further west along the coast are signs reading "Prehistoric Beehive Huts" where the owners of the land levy a small charge for viewing groups of fine *clocháin* with cahers, or encircling walls. The first group is *Cathair Connor* and the second is *Cathair na Máiríneach*. Within each of these cahers are *clocháin* of various sizes and in various stages of decay, many interlinked but some standing on their own. They are not prehistoric: most date from the early Christian period, and huts of this kind continued to be built into the early years of this century.

The principal archaeologist of Fahan, R.A.S. Macalister, identified hundreds of *clocháin* (or beehive huts) on this narrow strip between Fahan and Coumeenole. Faced with the number of buildings here, he went as far as to refer to the "City of Fahan". Commentators have been hard pressed to explain this extraordinary concentration of buildings. Local historian Doncha Ó Conchúir has suggested that those living in the *clocháin* may have been working on the land to the north-east presided over by the ringfort of Rahinnane. But the most likely explanation seems to me to be that advanced by Peter Harbison in his recent book, *Pilgrimage in Ireland* (1991). He suggests that the beehive huts are associated with the pilgrimage on the Saints' Road to the summit of Mount Brandon. These *clocháin* around Glanfahan, he believes, provided accommodation for pilgrims arriving by sea from the south to take part in the pilgrimage, or leaving to continue on the next stage of a western maritime pilgrimage. In particular, he suggests that the huts here "served as resting places for pilgrims awaiting the right weather to make the journey to the Skelligs as part of an extended pilgrimage".

Such an explanation appeals to me particularly because my researches in the 1970s supported the notion that the route of the Saints' Road may have extended south-west from Lateevebeg via St Brendan's Well in Kildurrihy and through Caherbullig to Glanfahan. I had in mind at the time a permanent settlement, but Harbison's suggestion that the beehive huts were temporarily occupied by pilgrims certainly makes sense.

The walker can rejoin the Dingle Way at Fahan after leaving Dunbeg and continue along the slope of Mount Eagle. It makes for a magnificent ramble on a good day, with the occasional lobster boat or trawler passing in the sea below and usually a cooling breeze off the sea. The track soon drops down into Glanfahan. Above farmhouses here turf tracks rise on the western side of the river to the summit of Mount Eagle. Judging by the depth to which the tracks are eroded, a great deal of turf must have been brought down in the past, and now they offer a good route to the top of the mountain, with great views of the sea and the Iveragh Peninsula.

Down below, the road from Fahan swings sharply right into the glen of Glanfahan and crosses a stream at a ford. Above, west of the bridge over the old road, the Dingle Way continues west, passing Cathair Murphy and *Cathair-fada-an-dorais*, the long caher of the door. At Slea Head the route dips down to the road. Here the Blaskets come into full view, and a little further on there is a viewing park.

The strand below is Coumeenole, a beautiful and sheltered place to sunbathe and perhaps to paddle, but unfortunately dangerous for bathing when the tide is on the ebb. A cargo boat, the *Ranga*, came to

grief here in March 1982; in the midst of a fierce storm all the members of the crew were rescued, half by helicopter, and half from the cliff above by breech's-buoy.

The headland here is Dunmore Head and, as the name suggests (*Dún Mór*, the big fort) it was a promontory fort. All that remains of the fort is a ditch and a wall, but certainly the area enclosed, within which stands an ogham stone, is large. Although *Mór* means large it is also the name of a pagan deity, who was married to Lir, the god of the sea, and who was a daughter of the sun. One story has it that the *dún* is named after her and that it was also called *Tigh Mhóire na Gréine*, the house of Mór of the sun. Another place traditionally associated with Mór is *Tigh Mhóire* in Vicarstown, her reputed grave, which lies in to the right off the road in the townland of Vicarstown, at the southern side of Dunquin.

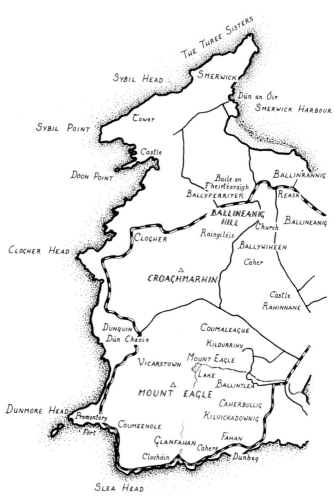

THE THREE SISTERS

SYBIL HEAD

SMERWICK

Dún an Óir
SMERWICK HARBOUR

SYBIL POINT

Tower

Castle

DOON POINT

Baile an
Fheirtéaraigh
BALLYFERRITER

BALLINRANNIG

REASK

BALLINEANIG
HILL

Church

BALLINEANIG

CLOGHER HEAD

CLOGHER

Raingiléis

BALLYWIHEEN

Caher

△
CROAGHMARHIN

Castle
RAHINNANE

DUNQUIN
Dún Chaoin

COUMALEAGUE

KILDURRIHY

Mount Eagle
Lake

VICARSTOWN

BALLINTLEA

△
MOUNT EAGLE

CAHERBULLIG

KILVICKADOWNIG

DUNMORE HEAD

Promontory
Fort

COUMEENOLE

GLANFAHAN

FAHAN

Cahers

Dunbeg

Clocháin

SLEA HEAD

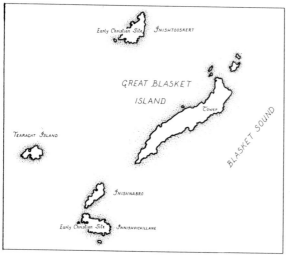

Early Christian Site   INISHTOOSKERT

GREAT BLASKET
ISLAND

Tower

BLASKET SOUND

TEARAGHT ISLAND

INISHNABRO

Early Christian Site   INNISHVICKILLANE

The Blaskets, Dunquin and Ballyferriter

O
N THE ROAD from Dunmore Head to Dunquin there is an unobstructed view of the western ocean. The varieties of evening light here are infinite: I have seen the sea like an endless sheet of beaten gold only an hour after displaying pure azure stippled with white; on other occasions I have seen thin yellow light change to pink and move through a range of colours to deep crimson and purple. When rain clouds move towards the coast, sunlight filters and beams from behind them: diffused, hazy light combines with strong shafts that are bright spots amidst advancing darkness.

Beautiful as the sea may be, it has often claimed lives – of fishermen and islanders and, most dramatically, of those on board a ship of the Spanish Armada. Just off Dunmore Head ships of the Armada sheltered near Beginish, the flattest of the Blasket Islands, in the treacherous Blasket Sound. The *San Juan de Ragusa* sank, but those on board were taken on to other ships. The *Santa Maria de la Rosa*, firing guns of distress, anchored in the sound on 1 October 1588, but she dragged her anchor, struck a rock and sank, one of the largest ships of the Armada to be lost. The sole survivor, Antonio de Monana, was the son of the ship's pilot, whom the captain had killed in a fit of rage when the ship was in its final moments. An underwater excavation was carried out on the wreck in 1968. Four hundred years after the Armada a monument commemorating the *Santa Maria de la Rosa* was erected in Dunquin overlooking the Blasket Sound. The sea between the islands and the mainland took its toll of Blasket islanders over the years, a fact and an ever-present danger which made a strong argument for moving to the mainland.

It was, inevitably, a hard life that was lived on the island, but in its later years it attracted the attention of scholars from outside and it gave birth to several remarkable books by islanders, books which have achieved a very wide international readership and which succeeded in uniquely representing the experience of people in a pre-feudal, pre-capitalist society.

The Great Blasket leaves a deep impression on many who visit it and the experience can be especially rewarding for those who have read those outstanding books written by a generation of islanders. The most notable of the books are *An tOileánach* (1929) – published in English translation as *The Islandman* (1937) – by Tomás Ó Criomhthain, *Fiche Bliain ag Fás* (1933) – *Twenty Years a-Growing* (1933) – by Muiris Ó Súilleabháin, and *Peig: A Scéal Féin* (1936) – *Peig* (1974) – by Peig Sayers. These books and others offer the best introduction to the Great Blasket. Much has been written about the islands and the life that was maintained there until evacuation in 1953, and the three main books have achieved a very important place in the national culture.

One of the islands, Inishvickillane, possesses an interesting early Christian settlement and there is also an early Christian site on Inishtooskert. Of more recent interest is the fact that Inishvickillane is owned by former Taoiseach (Prime Minister) Charles J. Haughey, who

has had a number of red deer brought to the island, where he has a house in which he stays quite often in the summer. Anyone wishing to visit Inishvickillane would need to seek his permission.

Inishvickillane and the Tearaght are breeding grounds for seabirds, most notably storm petrels, and in the Blaskets and the sea surrounding them many other seabirds are to be seen, such as terns, kittiwake, puffin, barnacle geese, fulmar, gannet and shearwaters. A pair of white eagles has recently been introduced to Inishvickillane.

It is not known for how long the islands were inhabited, but a story in the oral tradition concerned a Spanish woman whose body was washed ashore from a ship of the Spanish Armada on the strand of the Great Blasket, and who was buried at Castle Point.

Piaras Ferriter, the seventeenth-century leader of the resistance to English rule, had a castle on the island, where he took refuge from the English army. He was hidden for a time in a cave known to this day as Pierce's Cave.

The Ferriters, an Anglo-Norman family who had become completely gaelicised, owned the Blaskets, as well as a great deal of land on the peninsula. After Piaras Ferriter had been captured and executed, however, their estates were confiscated and the islanders from then on had to pay rents to English landlords. To pay their rents they sold livestock and fish at the market in Dingle. By 1756 there were five or six families living on the Great Blasket, but evictions and famine on the mainland drove many people to try to eke out existences on mountain slopes and in rough, rugged valleys, and some settled on several of the Blaskets, taking advantage of the availability of shellfish, sea-birds (they ate gannets in particular) and rabbits. By 1841 the population of the islands was 28 families (153 people). But the Great Famine soon reduced the numbers, and ten years later there were 19 families (97 people) there.

After the Famine fishing became the most important aspect of island life, and the islanders adopted the canvas-covered currach or *naomhóg*, which was light and manoeuverable, making it ideal for setting and drawing lobster pots. But after a few decades of relative prosperity the Blasket Island fishermen lost out to competition from larger boats.

The life of the island was a simple one based on a subsistence economy, and the islanders enjoyed the simple but rich pleasures of music, singing, dancing and storytelling. And it was its storytellers which brought the Great Blasket to wide national and international attention.

Tomás Ó Criomhthain (O'Crohan) was born in 1856; Peig Sayers in 1873; Muiris Ó Súilleabháin (O'Sullivan) in 1904. These were to become the three best-known storytellers from the island, recording a life that, even as it passed, seemed centuries old. Although often referred to as if these were the naive outpourings of uneducated peasants, their books demonstrated considerable skills and accomplishment, which is one of the reasons why they are still so readable today. As George Thomson, the Marxist classical scholar, wrote in *Island Home: The Blasket Heritage*:

> These authors were all versed to a greater or lesser degree in the art of storytelling. Their mode of speech and their outlook on life had been moulded by the traditional tales which they had inherited from past generations. What they did, therefore, was to select from their own experience a number of episodes which they had already cultivated as fireside tales and arrange them as a continuous narra-tive. In their hands, therefore, the transition from speech to writing was effected without a break. The magic of the fireside tale was car-ried over into print.

An important catalyst in the development of the Blasket authors was the presence on the island at various times of a number of scholars, including George Thomson and Robin Flower from England, Carl Marstrander from Norway, Marie Sjvestedt-Jonval from France and Carl von Sydow from Sweden.

Emigration, however, continued, and soon the island was almost entirely bereft of young people, who had followed members of their fam-ilies who had gone before them to Springfield, Massachussets. For those who remained much of the joy of life had gone with the young people, and when the government offered modern houses for them on the main-land they were inclined to accept the offer. By 1953 the Great Blasket was abandoned, and so it has remained, apart from occasional transient island-dwellers who have stayed for varying periods and provided a café/guesthouse service in one of the renovated Blasket homes. In 1993 a wonderful poem about the Blaskets won the first National Irish Poetry

Competition; written by David Quin, it is called "Pity the Islanders, *Lucht an Oileáin*", and it speaks memorably of the life that is now gone.

for they dwelt on a rock in the sea and not in a shining metropolis
and lived off the pick of the strand, the hunt of the hill, the fish in the sea,
the wool off sheep, and packets full of dollars; for they ate black pudding,

drank *sleadaí* squeezed from seaweed, treated themselves on Good
    Fridays
to tit-bits from the shore, and thought a man rich if he possessed two cows;
for they stuffed their pillows with puffins' feathers, and the sea roared

in their right ear and the north wind moaned in their left; for they were
    full
of sunlight and mist, wind and stone, rain and rock, but the Atlantic ocean
would not pay them a regular salary; and they did not fret about tumble
    driers

or grouse about the menu, for the wind would not let them strut, the
rain made them meek and the waves kept them low; for they feared vain-
    glory
and the evil eye, chewed bits of seaweed and prayed to the mother of God;

for their enemies were bailiffs, big fat trawlers, mainland shopkeepers
and crows after hens; for they made nothing fit for museum or art gallery
and uttered proverbs that came up from Cro Magnon man; for they lived

before Descartes, Newton, Freud, de Sade and Marx, invented no novel
    machine
or vice, and never discovered the multiple orgasm; for they lacked
    ambition,
built into the earth not the sky, and did not rob and plunder or scatter

corpses in their wake; for they lived before the age of trivia
and never made it to the age of anxiety, and did not suffer ennui because
there was turf to be cut; for they did not rush into the future,

leaving their hearts behind them, because they had no future.
Praise the islanders, *lucht an Oileáin*, for they were a fair people
who pelted the stranger with blessings and the bailiffs with volleys of stones;

for they were a gentle people, who twisted puffins' necks, patted babies'
   heads
and split the skulls of seals; for they were like the children of one mother
   with twenty
steps between each house; for they were a quiet people, who never

stopped talking, full of malice and affection, whose delights were tea
and tobacco, a big ship on the waves, a donkey on the loose, a battle
of tongues, a boatful of rabbits, a dance, a story, a song in the dead of
   night;

for they were as mournful as wet sheep and as bright as gannets,
were pagans who trusted in God, rubbed seal oil on their wounds,
welcomed wrecks but prayed for the corpses, and loved to fill their bellies

with the breeze that flows from the west; for they broke their backs with
   loads
of fish and sand, turf and lobsters, and leant on walls to bask in the sun;
for their stage was not the city, nation or world, but the village, the island

and the neighbouring parishes, which are about the right size for a
   human being.
When they strolled beneath the Milky Way their laughter did not pol-
   lute the night,
for they kept their boats high on the waves and their roofs low to the
   ground

and were grateful for seals when God withheld pigs.

The mainland harbour for the islanders was at Dunquin, where the
pier – which is signposted from the main road – is surrounded by cliffs
of coloured silurian rock, rich in fossils and as soft, in parts, as clay. At
the bottom of a steep and winding concrete pathway, canoes rest on their
stands like giant black beetles. Frail as they look, with their tarred canvas over light frames, they were used to carry everything from livestock
to building materials between the mainland and the islands.

Dunquin is the centre of attention for visitors interested in the Irish
language. Indeed, the language is the central factor in the identity of the
western part of the peninsula and particularly of Dunquin where, in

1970, there was a long, hard battle to keep the local school open. A national focus at the time in the struggle to give Irish its rightful place, the battle was won and twenty-five pupils were attending the school in 1993. To its attraction as a centre of the Irish language has also been added the presence of an *An Óige* hostel.

Kruger's pub, which is well signposted, is the main social centre and it is named after "Kruger" Kavanagh, the late owner, a renowned and colourful character who spun magnificent yarns, especially about his time in the United States, and whose name came from his expressions of support for the Afrikaners in the Boer War. Modernised in the 1980s, it is a pub that was frequented in its time by writers and artists, including Brendan Behan, who wrote first in Irish. It has also hosted the launches of many books by local authors.

In Dunquin a very large Blasket Island interpretative centre has been built by the Office of Public Works on a site of 47 acres between the road and the sea, and it provides information, displays and video shows about every aspect of the Blaskets. Constructed around an axis of a 60-metre-long corridor which leads at the end to a large window looking out on the Great Blasket, it has rooms and display areas of different shapes and sizes leading off this substantial corridor, and a café. Outside, a carpark provides space for 156 cars and 6 coaches. Its construction in 1992–93 at a cost of about £4 million was the subject of considerable controversy, and coincided with similar controversy in relation to other proposed interpretative centres in other parts of the country. Nationally and internationally, environmentalists, botanists, naturalists, artists and writers opposed the siting of these interpretative centres, but the proponents of the centres, the Office of Public Works, insisted that the sites chosen were the only viable sites, and that the centres would provide significant local employment. This latter argument was of forceful relevance in Dunquin, where nothing was closer to the hearts of most people than the prospect of local employment for their sons and daughters. As it turned out, the promises of the numbers of jobs were nowhere near realised, and many of those who had vigorously supported the proposed centre find that they now share the reservations of those who opposed it. Conversely, some of those who opposed it are keen to ensure that, now that it does exist, it is as lively a centre of activity as possible.

The only physical remnant of the filming of David Lean's film, *Ryan's Daughter,* is in Dunquin. The left turn after the interpretative centre on the road northwards leads via a path to the ruins of what was the film schoolhouse. Those who have seen the film may well recognise the cut-stone walls, but closer inspection reveals that some of the features of the building are of fibreglass. Above the "schoolhouse" is the holy well of St Gobnait, neatly dressed with stone and with a fine stone head sculpted by Cliona Cussen. On the right-hand side of the road to Ballyferriter is the youth hostel.

Back at the crossroads near Kruger's a bohareen leads inland past the church and into *Gleann Mór*. The cluster of outhouses on the left is the remains of an old clachan, showing the characteristic arrangement of houses at different angles. Above is a modern mansion built for Dolores O'Riordan of the Cranberries at enormous expense, and soon abandoned by her. Further on the bohareen becomes a track which leads towards the *Mám Clasach*, the pass over to Ventry. On a fine day this can make for a pleasant short walk. On the right of the track beside a stream a few stones amidst the undergrowth are all that remains of a community that numbered over one hundred people in 1841; like a number of small communities on the peninsula it did not survive the Famine: by 1851 it was deserted.

Further on up *Gleann Mór* are altogether earlier remains which probably date to the Early Bronze Age. On the southern slopes of the valley is a megalithic wedge-tomb, largely buried in the bog. On the northern side of the stream is an old field system which may predate the bog and belong to the same period as the tomb. A standing stone near this field system has beside it another megalithic structure which may well be the remains of another tomb. In amongst the field system are several circular enclosures, a cairn, and what appears to be a cist grave.

If the road between Dunmore Head and Dunquin provides a magnificent view out over the expanse of water, Clogher Strand, between Dunquin and Ballyferriter, is one of the best places to stand on the shoreline and watch the movement of water. Its moods vary, the weather often conveying with its strong swell a warning of storms in the offing; its moods vary also with the light playing on the water below the dark mass of Clogher Head, an outcrop formed by massive volcanic eruption. The sea erupts here too at times and when storms hit from the west waves crashing on the rocks tower high, their heavy spray spreading like a thick cloud inland. Not a place for swimming, Clogher Strand is best visited towards dusk and on days when storms are approaching or gales are already blowing. The colours of the sandstone here are characteristic of the area, and the same colours may be seen in the stone of Kilmalkedar church.

On the approach to Ballyferriter a site on the right of the road is marked on some Ordnance Survey maps as a stone circle; however, it is only an old beehive hut from which all but a few stones have been removed. There are, in fact, no stone circles on the Dingle Peninsula, even though they are very numerous in parts of Kerry to the south and east, and in neighbouring County Cork.

Ballyferriter is an important and lively centre for many people holidaying in the west. There are numerous chalets and other rented accommodation in the area; there are pubs, hotels, restaurants, a church, post office and police station. Here, too, is a small museum, an exhibition featuring aspects of the historical, archaeological and cultural heritage of the peninsula. Near by are fine beaches at *Béal Bán* and the Wine Strand, and at the Wine Strand is a large development of holiday homes.

Like so many parts of the peninsula, the Ballyferriter area is perfect countryside for the walker. Half a mile along the road north out of Ballyferriter is a bohareen to the left signposted to *Béal Bán*. The strand is about a mile from the main road. To the left along the strand is a cluster of houses; about 500 yards along the road here a right turn leads to *Dún an Óir*, the fort of gold, scene of an infamous massacre in 1580. Those travelling by car from Ballyferriter village should take the Dunquin road and turn to the right after about half a mile where there are signposts to the *Dún an Óir* hotel. At a junction turn right and then right again for the fort.

The promontory here was originally an Iron Age promontory fort, but it was given new defences in 1580 by a force of about six hundred Italians and Spaniards under the command of Sebastiano di San Giuseppe of Bologna, after some earlier preparatory work by James Fitzmaurice. This intervention was an attempt to back Irish revolt against British rule with foreign military aid, and the English responded forcefully; although there was a specifically Irish element, it was more than anything else an incident in a general European struggle, in which the English were determined to show their resolve to resist attack through the "back door" of Ireland.

In early November 1580 Admiral Winter's fleet arrived in Smerwick

Harbour and Lord Grey of Wilton, the English Lord Deputy, marched through the peninsula and arrived at *Dún an Óir* with eight hundred soldiers. The defence of the fort was incompetently organised, Lord Grey's troops were able to move in close, and on the third day the Spanish surrendered. Both then and since there has been much argument as to the terms of the surrender – whether they had been led to believe their lives would be spared or not. In a letter to Queen Elizabeth, Lord Grey explained what followed the surrender:

> I sent in certain gentlemen to see their weapons and armures layed downe and to gard the munitions and victaile their left for spoile: Then put I in certeyn bandes who streight fell to execution. There were 600 slayne: munition and vittaile great store, though much wasted through the disorder of the Souldier, which in that furie could not be helped. Those that I gave life unto, I have bestowed upon the Capteines and gentlemen.

The Queen's response was to congratulate him on being chosen as an instrument of God's glory, but to criticise him for the fact that he had allowed some to remain alive.

The few Irish in the garrison were dealt with more ceremoniously – they were hanged; an English Catholic and two prominent Irish

Catholics had each of their arms and legs broken in three places and were not hung until the next day. Bishop Hugh Bradie of Meath called it "the most profitable service achieved since Her Majesty wore the crown".

Heated debate continued through the centuries as to whether Lord Grey had made promises of safe conduct to the defenders or not. Even T.J. Westropp, the archaeologist of the promontory forts, writing in the early years of this century, devoted most of his text on *Dún an Óir* to a spirited defence of Lord Grey. It has been argued, too, that too much attention has been paid to it, that it was only one of a number of such incidents at the time. Certainly there had been other massacres, such as that at Carrigafoyle in April of the same year, but the Smerwick massacre served a particular propaganda purpose for the English in warning off any future attempts at invasion from Europe in support of Irish rebels.

The massacres were not the most horrific features of this period: of all those that died in the war, comparatively few died by the sword. The strategy successfully employed by the English was to contain the revolt within Munster, where they applied a scorched earth policy. The people's cattle were taken, their houses and corn burned; and they starved. Those that did not flee were liable to be killed: and so they hid in the hills. The Four Masters recorded that in 1583 "the lowing of a cow, or the voice of the ploughman, could scarcely be heard from Dunquin to Cashel". The ordinary people were caught between an English administration determined to establish its power by any means necessary and the old feudal lords who wished to hold on to their powers and freedom.

A memorial was erected on the site in 1980.

To the west of the fort rise the three peaks known as the Three Sisters, which are worth visiting on a fine day for the view alone. On *Binn Diarmada*, the highest of the peaks, is a precipitous ledge about which two stories are told: one is that Diarmuid and Gráinne, figures in one of the best known Irish legends, slept here while being pursued through the country; the other is that one of the Fianna named Diarmuid stood watch here when the invasion was anticipated that resulted in the Battle of Ventry. In more recent times it was over the Three Sisters that Lindbergh flew in *The Spirit of St Louis* in 1927 when he first reached sight of land after crossing the Atlantic. He signalled a fishing canoe north of the Three Sisters, flew over the westernmost of the three hills and continued south-east via *Mám na Gaoithe* above Ventry, on towards Valentia, where news of his arrival was immediately conveyed by the radio station to the international news media. From Valentia he continued to his triumphant landing in Paris.

There is a crossroads about 500 yards further along the road past the fort. About one-and-a-half miles (2.4 kilometres) further on the road swings sharply left; later it swings right towards the *Dún an Óir* hotel and Ballyoughteragh.

Ballyoughteragh, or *Baile Uachtarach*, the upper townland, features in *The Boycotting Song*, one of the very few songs which refer to the evictions which were a dominant fact of life in the 1880s. Landlords at that time evicted, or tried to evict, many tenants who could not pay their rent, and the struggle by the tenant farmers to defend their livings was a bitter one. The tactic of boycotting was used to great effect: anyone who co-operated with the landlords or police or who took over houses and lands from which tenants had been evicted incurred the violent contempt of their neighbours; publicans and other business people who provided for the needs of the landlords and their agents found themselves instantly isolated by the rest of the community. The song concerns policemen in Ballyoughteragh who were given two cows by Lord Ventry. There is an ironic restraint in the song: although it states that the cows just wandered off, in fact they were taken by local people and driven over a cliff to their deaths.

> The Bail' Uachtarach peelers were boycotted well
> For not one in the parish would them anything sell,
> So out of sheer pity those quellers of rows
> Received from Lord Ventry two black Kerry cows.

On the way home the peelers stop for a drink in a roadside shebeen, leaving the cows unattended.

> The peelers were drinking 't is drink to their heart,
> The "Kerrys" outside got a notion to start,
> One started to the east and another to the west,
> An' the peelers and bailiffs were taking their rest.

When they discover their loss, the peelers search high and low. But "Not a sign of those 'Kerrys' was seen anywhere/Like the witches of old they went off in the air."

A green track leads uphill from Ballyoughteragh to the ruins of a tower built as a look-out post at the end of the eighteenth century when it was feared that Napoleon's forces would invade. It stands on a height above Sybil Point and from it similar towers on the Great Blasket and at Ballydavid Head were visible and could be communicated with.

Sybil Point and Sybil Head are said to be named after Sybil Lynch, and near Doon Point a stump of masonry is all that remains of Sybil Castle, also known as Ferriter's Castle. In fact, they were named earlier than her time but the story is worth recording. The Ferriters – originally le Furetur – were a Norman family who settled here in the thirteenth century. Sybil Lynch of Galway eloped with one of the Ferriters and was pursued by her father. She hid in a cave while her father laid siege to the castle, but when the fight was over it was found that the sea had swept through the cave and washed her away.

Doon Point is another of the many coastal promontory forts. Extending for more than 500 yards (460 metres), it is 328 feet (100 metres) wide at its landward end, and it tapers to a sharp point at its western extremity. The neck of this promontory is defended by a series of banks and fosses, and here a later castle or tower-house was built in the fifteenth or sixteenth century. Unusually for a site of this kind, it has in effect two necks, a second narrowing and a second series of banks and ditches occurring about 515 feet (157 metres) west of the first. Within the western enclosure are the faint traces of many hut-sites. Only a stump of masonry of the tower-house remains.

Below Doon Point lies Ferriter's Cove, and here in the cliff-face can be seen a series of shell middens, which are the earliest known archaeological remains on the Dingle Peninsula. Excavated during the 1980s, the site showed the characteristic piles of shells, together with hearths and charcoal, and it yielded finds of wild pig and red deer bones, fish bones and stone tools. Indeed, the stone tools found here seem to have been made just a few miles south near Dunquin. Carbon dating places this site between 3670 and 3240 BC, in the late mesolithic/early neolithic period, and it is definitely mesolithic in type.

Visible from Doon Point and Ferriter's Castle is *Dún an Óir* hotel. Its

Reask, Gallarus, Kilmalkedar
and the Saints' Road

F<small>ROM</small> B<small>ALLYFERRITER THE</small> road north and east leads into an area which was a cradle of early Christian civilisation. Here, at the western edge of Europe, a new way was forged in the course of the fifth to eighth centuries and a lifestyle was developed which was to contribute to the remarkable and extensive Irish missionary movement of later centuries throughout continental Europe.

One can get an idea of what an intensive development took place here by looking at the concentration of early Christian settlements. One mile from *Raingiléis*, which we visited in the last chapter, lies the excavated site of Reask; one-and-a-half miles from Reask is the cross-slab of a settlement at Lateevemanagh. A mile from Lateevemanagh is Templenacloonagh, and both Kilcolman and St Manchan's lie about a half-mile over the hill. The oratory of Gallarus is only half a mile from Templenacloonagh and a mile from Kilmalkedar church. The settlement at *Cráilí* is less than a mile-and-a-half from Kilmalkedar, and Reenconnell is less than a mile distant. Ten early ecclesiastical sites within a small triangle of land.

There are about sixty such sites on the Dingle Peninsula, including its islands, and these offer substantial evidence of a cultural and religious flowering in the fifth to eighth centuries. It may be that some of the sites – particularly those on islands – were chosen initially out of a wish to get closer to God by getting further from human society. But many of the settlements were situated in the midst of fertile land where there was a considerable secular population, and most of the early Christians were probably engaged in pastoral work rather than being isolated hermits. Given the evidence of the preceding era, the Iron Age, it is likely that the early missionaries were attracted to this area because it had a developed and stable society rather than because it was a remote backwater.

Today we can walk through the countryside and see the modest remains of what must in some sense at least have been a golden age. Access to all of the sites is easy and one soon becomes familiar with the similarities and differences evident in the styles of the cross-slabs, the enclosure walls, the *clocháin* and oratories. Many of the structures and stones of these settlements have been submerged as the ground level has risen, but at Reask excavation and conservation allow us to see the characteristic layout of these sites.

The road from Ballyferriter to the north passes a creamery on the left and immediately swings sharply right over a bridge and past Bric's recently rebuilt pub and guesthouse; the next right turn leads to Reask.

A Christian settlement of the fifth to seventh century, it was at first a very simple settlement within an enclosure wall consisting of a wooden structure in the central area and probably the two small single *clocháin*, and a lintel grave cemetery marked by inscribed pillar-stones with a

small slab-shrine and possibly a wooden oratory. The pair of smaller conjoined *clocháin* in the western sector was built a little later. Then the small stone oratory was erected on top of some of the early graves and the wall dividing sanctuary and cemetery from the habitation area was built; the two large conjoined *clocháin* were erected where part of the enclosure wall had stood and a new portion of enclosing wall was constructed around them; a paved way was made between these huts and the oratory through an entrance in the dividing wall.

The early occupation of the site was, it seems, by one or two "eremetic" holy men, rejecting the world and seeking to transcend the physical in search of spiritual discovery and truth. Later, in about the seventh or eighth century, the development was of a monastic kind and lasted probably until it was deserted in about the twelfth century. In this period it may well have been more a clustered habitation site than a place specifically dedicated to religious pursuits. After it had been abandoned the cemetery and oratory were used as a calluragh or *ceallúnach* for the burial of unbaptised children. Part of the habitation area was made into plots for grazing and tillage and some of the structures were used for animal shelters.

The Reask excavation has produced valuable evidence towards an understanding of this kind of site which is such a feature of the western coast of Ireland. Anyone seeking a more detailed description of the site should read Tom Fanning's report, *Excavation of an Early Christian Cemetery and Settlement at Reask, County Kerry* (Proceedings of the Royal Irish Academy Vol 81, C, No. 3).

After visiting the site thirsty visitors can repair to Bric's pub where, as in all pubs in the west of the peninsula, they can exercise whatever command they have of the Irish language. The road beside the bridge opposite the pub leads to a fine bathing strand at Ballinrannig; those who linger on the beach into the evening are likely to hear the distinctive sound of the curlew for, while it frequents many of the coastal areas and hills of the peninsula, this is one of its favourite haunts.

From Reask the main road continues east; it passes a turn to the left with a signpost to Gallarus oratory and then rises to sharp bends at Lateevemore. At the height of the road it swings sharply left, but on the right an old track pursues a route along the foot of the hill to Lateevebeg. Lined with fuchsia, which grows prolifically in the warm, wet climate, it is the pilgrimage path known as the Saints' Road, and it has now become part of the Dingle Way.

In early Christian and medieval times, one of Ireland's most important places of pilgrimage was Mount Brandon, and certain routes to the mountain summit became known as pilgrimage paths. Eventually one particular pathway became established as the Saints' Road and was recorded in the nineteenth century on the Ordnance Survey maps as extending from Lateevebeg, through Kilmalkedar, and up to the summit of Mount Brandon.

In the early Christian period, the most notable settlement of all on the south-west coast was Skellig Michael, where a monastery of beehive huts clung to precarious ledges on the steep-sided island. For the people from Skellig Michael taking part in the pilgrimage, Ventry would have been the most convenient landing place. There were also many early Christian settlements on the Iveragh Peninsula, and the people who lived in these could make the short crossing of Dingle Bay to take part in the pilgrimage. Wells in Kildurrihy and Maumanorig, both near Ventry, are dedicated to Saint Brendan and may have been starting-points for some pilgrims.

It may be, also, that the Saints' Road came from further south, from the major centre of population in the early Christian period at Fahan. There was certainly a continuous road from Fahan, via Kilvickadownig, Kildurrihy and Rahinnane to Lateevebeg.

Peter Harbison, in *Pilgrimage in Ireland* (1991) has suggested that pilgrims came from far and wide, taking part in a western maritime pilgrimage which extended along the Atlantic coastline of the west of Ireland and Scotland, and as far as Iceland, Greenland and even North America. The early Christian settlements that are such a feature of the Dingle Peninsula were, he considers, created by and for pilgrims rather than ascetic monks.

> It is the Dingle peninsula that provides our most striking archaeological confirmation of the former existence of a western maritime pilgrimage in that its pilgrimage road to the cult centre on Mount Brandon starts not at the landward end of the peninsula but near a fine landing place close to its western extremity. The wide variety of the peninsula's stone monuments such as beehive huts, cross-bearing pillars and ogham stones really only begins to make sense when seen in conjunction with the pilgrimage to Mount Brandon.

Many of the early Christian sites on the peninsula lie on the line of the Saints' Road, and at Lateevemanagh, near its start, is a field called *Gort na Croise*, the field of the cross, in which are the slight remains of an early Christian settlement. All that is visible now is a very small mound from which projects a stone slab incised with an equal-armed cross, simply and neatly made without any enclosing circle or other decoration. Near by at Maumanorig another equal-armed cross decorates the stone dedicated in ogham to Colman the Pilgrim, and Harbison suggests that both equal-armed crosses and ogham inscriptions have a special association with pilgrimage.

Lateeve, or *Leataoibh*, is a simple descriptive name, meaning the side of a hill, and this hill offers a pleasant walk, with good views when the day is clear, along its ridge or over to St Manchan's Church on the other side. At Lateevemore, where there is a group of houses, a bohareen leads off the lower bend in the road and passes St Ita's National School, now disused, above which is *Tobar na gCapall*, which was credited with curing horses and which now supplies water through a piped system to many houses in the district.

Further along this bohareen another, very narrow bohareen crosses; just before this little crossroads, in fields on the left, stand the remains of *Teampall na Cluanach* (Templenacloonagh), another early Christian settlement. Two early Christian buildings and three cross-slabs are enclosed within a cashel wall; the more southerly of the two ruined structures is an oratory, measuring about 16 feet (5 metres) by 12 feet (3.5 metres); the other was probably a church. The two cross-inscribed pillars are unusual and feature Latin, Syrian and Greek crosses; there is also a cross-inscribed boulder lying on the wall of the building in the north of the enclosure. Within the enclosure, too, are piles of stones which may have been two conjoined huts. The site is known locally as *Teampall Bán*.

From the bends at Lateevemore the main road continues along the foot of the hill to Ballynana – *Baile na nÁth*, the townland of the height. A left turn leads to Gallarus. There is a small parking space at the side of the road, with a neatly hedged pathway leading to the oratory; access here is free. Alternatively, one can enter the site further west along this road, where a privately owned visitor centre has been built.

Gallarus oratory is a most perfect early stone building; it represents the height of dry-stone corbelling and is thought for this reason to be later than most oratories. Its date has in fact been the subject of much argument. Most oratories were built in the seventh and eighth centuries, but the refinement of its construction and its arched east window suggest

that it was built much later. The cross-slab beside the oratory is typical of seventh-century settlements, but this oratory probably succeeded an earlier one on this site. The name of Gallarus is open to several interpretations, but one possibility is that it signifies a "house for foreigners", referring to the people who came from outside the area to take part in the pilgrimage.

The method of building is derived from that used in megalithic tombs and *clocháin*: flat stones are placed so that, as the walls rise, each level projects slightly further in than the previous one. As the walls curve inwards they meet at the top and are capped off with large stones. The stones of the walls are laid at a slight angle, lower at the outside than the inside, allowing the water to run off. The effectiveness of the method may be seen at Gallarus which is as firm and dry as the day it was built. Its shape is similar to that of an upturned boat it has a door in the west wall which is wider at the base than the top, and a window in the east wall. The oratory's position gives it a commanding view of Smerwick Harbour, whose brightness on a sunny day is well caught in Seamus Heaney's poem, "In Gallarus Oratory".

> You can still feel the community pack
> This place: it's like going into a turfstack,
> A core of old dark walled up with stone
> A yard thick. When you're in it alone
> You might have dropped, a reduced creature
> To the heart of the globe. No worshipper
> Would leap up to his God off this floor.
> Founded there like heroes in a barrow
> They sought themselves in the eye of their King
> Under the black weight of their own breathing.
> And how he smiled on them as out they came,
> The sea a censer, and the grass a flame.

A different aspect of the view of Smerwick Harbour is illustrated in a story associated with the nearby Gallarus Castle, which was one of the seats of the Knights of Kerry. The last of the Fitzgeralds to live there demanded to be taken from his deathbed and placed before a window from which he could watch the wild storm that was raging. His last words were: "'Tis just the day for a Geraldine to die." The castle is the best preserved of the tower-houses on the peninsula, all of which were similarly designed. A four-storey rectangular castle which still has its vaulted roof, it was probably built in the fifteenth century and was occupied by the Fitzgeralds until 1688. It can be reached by taking the road downhill from the oratory and the second bohareen to the right.

Near by is a restaurant and an approved camping and caravan site which offers the opportunity to camp in this beautiful area which is so rich in antiquities and close to safe bathing strands. The road uphill from the oratory leads to the main road and a left turn towards Kilmalkedar. Just after a side-road to the left, on the left-hand side is the fine site of *Cathair Deargáin*. This is a stone fort with a single defensive wall about 30 yards (27 metres) across and 9 feet (2.7 metres) thick, enclosing a group of *clocháin*, three of which are interlinked. It is a good example of the kind of homestead occupied by the ruling families of the early Christian period, and it has recently been restored by the Office of Public Works. Its local name is *Cróidhte na Cathrach*, the huts of the caher. The *clocháin* are of different sizes, one being so small it must have been a dog kennel. On the north-western side the cashel wall is as high as 9 feet (2.7 metres).

On the left a little beyond Caherdargan stands the ruined Chancellor's House, a single-storey two-roomed dwelling house of the fifteenth century. What makes this building and St Brendan's House, beside the

church in Kilmalkedar, remarkable is that early dwelling houses, with the exception of the *clocháin,* were almost always built of wood or wattles and few rectangular stone houses have survived.

The house belonged to the Chancellor of the Diocese of Ardfert, and is an indication of the significance of this parish within the diocese. A Protestant Chancellor was resident in Kilmalkedar as late as 1864, though not in this building, and he went by the name of Chancellor Swindall, which may well have had a Dickensian appropriateness. On behalf of the Protestant Church he collected tithes from the peasants, who were almost all Roman Catholic. The tithes charged were punitive and hit the poor particularly hard by placing a levy on crops but not on cattle. Usurers profited from the system, charging high interest rates – known as "Kerry bonds" – on loans to pay the tithe. In many parts of the country there was resistance, often combined with opposition to the land enclosures which were a feature of the century from 1750 to 1850. In this area there were attacks on collectors by the "Whiteboys" – so called on account of their wearing white shirts and white cockades. Tralee gaol was attacked and prisoners liberated; but the periodic outbursts were violently put down by the landlords' militia, notably under the direction of Lord Kenmare. Late in the eighteenth century a large protest in Dingle was suppressed by the militia, and the many demonstrators killed came from a wide range of townlands on the peninsula.

Entering Kilmalkedar the road passes between two stones known as the Thief's and the Cow's Stones, though the westerly one is now buried. On the right stands the church, beside it, St Brendan's House, the presbytery; and in fields near by are a *bullán* and an oratory. In the field below the church on the opposite side of the road a simple cross-slab stands beside a well. Just below the churchyard an intriguing chamber built into a thick wall is known as "Poll Jo". A small cross near this structure suggests that this primitive cell may be the earliest evidence of Christian settlement in Kilmalkedar. Perhaps it is the first dwelling-place of Maolceadair, the founder of the settlement; his lonely example inspired others to come, and gradually a community developed.

The church is a fine example of Irish Romanesque: the nave was built in the mid-twelfth century and the chancel added a little later. The internal measurements of the nave are 8.2 metres long by 5.2 metres wide; the

chancel is 4.9 metres long and 3.5 metres wide, and the walls are about
4.3 metres high. Nothing remains of the roof, which was corbelled.

Early churches were almost always built of wood, stone being regarded as a foreign building medium; and *derthech* or *duirthech*, an Irish word
for church or oratory, means "oak-house". When stone began to be used,
characteristics of wooden building methods were often carried over into
the new medium. Here, the finials at the top of the west gable recall protruding cross-beams; and the antae, which are the protrusions at either
side of the west gable, also illustrate the imitation of wooden building
features. Architecturally it is an original mixture, combining outside
influences and local features, and its multicoloured local stone giving layers of green, gold, purple and brown.

The stone head above the doorway supposedly represents the founder
of the church; and on the antae at each of the four corners are animal
heads. Over the inside of the door is a fine bull's head, and two other animal heads are placed either side of the east window. The ball designs on
the outside of the doorway represent the decades of the rosary; and the
inclined jambs show the continued influence of the earlier stone
churches and oratories.

Inside the church the "alphabet stone" suggests a Christian teaching
settlement of the seventh century. Originally a tombstone – it bears, like
the cross pillar at Reask, an abbreviated inscription of "Domine" and a
cross – it was adapted for teaching the alphabet. The letters are seventh
century Roman and include the abbreviation for *et*.

Kilmalkedar was a centre of Christianity and scholarship. In the territory of the *Ciarraighe*, Ardfert was the principal church and it was associated with St Brendan. The evidence in the territory of the *Corca
Dhuibhne* is less conclusive, but everything points towards Kilmalkedar
and its founder, Maolceadair. It may have been chosen as a centre
because of its proximity to the pre-Christian religious symbol of Mount
Brandon and because Kilmalkedar itself was the main pagan centre in
the area. A remarkable aspect of the churchyard is the survival there of
pagan stones; and elements of the pagan religion were never wholly suppressed but were continued in Christianised forms.

St Brendan probably never set foot on the Dingle Peninsula, at least
on that part which lies south and west of Mount Brandon. The principal

founding father of Christianity in this area was Maolceadair, but the first bishop of Kerry in the eleventh century was from Ardfert and he imposed the cult of Brendan on the peninsula, including Kilmalkedar. However, in the following century there may have been a resurgence of local autonomy, and the building of the church here at Kilmalkedar perhaps reflects a revival of the cult of the local saint, Maolceadair.

The east window of the church is known as *Cró na Snáthaide*, or the eye of the needle. On Easter Sunday local people made nine clockwise circuits of the churchyard, keeping count by throwing pebbles on one particular grave. Similar forms of "*turas*", "round" and "patron" or "pattern" exist in many parts of Ireland, though very many have died out in the last hundred years, and they derive originally from pagan ritual. In *Corca Dhuibhne* the crust of Christianity over early religion seems especially thin.

The east window, a holed stone in the church and holed stones in the graveyard symbolise regeneration and resemble the Indian *yoni* stones; in addition cures are associated with some stones. The *deisiol* or sunwise round encircling the site was an important element in the animistic worship of trees, wells and stones. Such practices were denounced by the fifth century Council of Arles, but the early Christians in Ireland were forced to make accommodations. St Patrick adopted the *deisiol* round when consecrating the site of his cathedral in Armagh, as did St Senan at Scattery Island.

The tall holed stone in the graveyard bears an ogham inscription. Another stone in the graveyard has been described as a sundial but its

shape, position and design seem inappropriate. Others have described it as a "scratch dial", indicating times of services. On one side it features a *tau* or T-shaped cross. The overall design is exceptionally well executed and it is holed, though the hole does not penetrate to the other side of the stone. Another feature of the graveyard's fascinating mixture of pagan and Christian is one of the very few large early crosses in Kerry, neatly carved out of conglomerate rock. In the lane behind the church is a tiny gem of an oratory. Possibly the oldest of all the oratories, its structure stands firm despite the fact that a tree used to grow from its roof.

Another, larger oratory lies in a field above the road about 300 metres to the west. It is surrounded by a modern wall, its roof has fallen in and it is supported internally by a modern arch. It pales by comparison with Gallarus, but it is nevertheless a good example of an oratory and is certainly earlier than Gallarus.

Although this oratory and the presbytery beside the church have been named after St Brendan, it is almost certain that St Maolceadair was the principal monk here. The *Martyrology of Donegall* records his death:

AD 636. – Maolcethair, Son of the King of Uladh of Cill
Melchedair, near the shore of the sea to the west of Brandon Hill.
He was of the race of Fiatach Finn, Monarch of Érinn.

Why he should have come here from Ulster at a time of strict tribal divisions is explained by the fact that he was of a kindred tribe to the *Corca Dhuibhne*. As a king's son he would have been a natural choice for the principal priest in the region.

Despite strong tradition about Brendan at Kilmalkedar, Mount Brandon, Brandon Creek, *Seana Cill* and *Faiche na Manach*, it is unlikely that he was associated with the church in *Corca Dhuibhne* in his lifetime, since he was of the *Ciarraighe*. Two more likely contenders for the role of leading the growth of monasticism in the area are Maolceadair and Fionán Cam, who was a member of the *Corca Dhuibhne*. Fionán – called Cam on account of his squint – is associated primarily with the Iveragh Peninsula and the Skellig: the *Corca Dhuibhne* were divided in two by Dingle Bay (less of a division in practice than that of mountain ranges). The occupants of the Dingle Peninsula were the *Aos Iorrus Tuiscirt* and those of Iveragh, the *Aos Iorruis Deiscirt*; and it seems that Fionán worked mostly amongst the people of the southern peninsula, though there is one association with him on the Dingle Peninsula, at Kinard. Later, the barony of *Corca Dhuibhne* came to be confined to the northern peninsula.

In the medieval reorganisation of church administration, the tribal divisions between the *Ciarraighe* and the *Corca Dhuibhne* were maintained, and a special status was reserved for Kilmalkedar. But at some point in the rewriting of church history Brendan was adopted posthumously as the central symbolic figure of the region, displacing Maolceadair and Fionán.

In a field behind the house nearest to the church there is a *bullán*. This is similar to the *bulláin* in Kildurrihy and Dingle; but it has sunk into the ground and is called St Brendan's Keelers, from *cilorn*, meaning coolers, and tradition has it that it was used for separating cream from milk. A story is told involving this stone about a magical cow, the "*Glas Gaibhneach*", which is told in various versions in many parts of the country. There are several versions here, but all agree that the cow produced an inexhaustible supply of milk. A vessel only had to be placed under her and she filled it, and when nobody came she milk herself into the *bullán*. But one time a mischievous person placed a sieve under her: the milk flowed, but when she looked to see if the vessel was full, she was distressed to see the milk wasted on the ground as it ran away in rivulets. Such was her distress, say some, that she kicked up her heels and bounded off out of Ireland altogether, never to return. Others say she died on the spot. There is a reflection in the story about this magical cow of the female deities of supernatural plenty, such as Anu, earth mother and goddess of the *Tuatha Dé Danainn*.

St Brendan's House, just over the stream north of the church, was built at about the same time as the Chancellor's House – the fifteenth century – but it is larger and better preserved. As John O'Donovan wrote in the *Ordnance Survey Letters*, it is "one of the very few dwelling houses of the ancient Irish which the hand of envious time has spared for us". It had two storeys and the supports of the wooden upper floor are clearly visible. The building method is rugged: thick walls tapering as they rise. On one of its upper window-ledges a kestrel was perched on the unforgettable occasion when I first entered it.

The most notable walk to be taken from Kilmalkedar, and for historical reasons the most notable on the peninsula, is on the route of the old pilgrimage path, the Saints' Road, which continues over the hill to the north-east and down to an early Christian settlement at *Cráilí*, then to Ballybrack, from where it rises to the summit of Mount Brandon. A stone-paved track, bordered on the left by thick fuchsia hedges, leads from beside St Brendan's House up towards the hill. Soon there are fuchsia hedges on either side and as the track turns towards the left the hedges press closer together; a stream runs beside the path and in May foxgloves and birdseye speedwell grow here. Turning off to the right at a gate and heading straight uphill, the Saints' Road leaves the fuchsia behind and narrows. For some distance it is quite clearly distinguishable, paved with stones and bordered with gorse and heather. It peters out, but its local name, "the low way", gives the clue to the route, which passes over the lowest point of the shallow saddle of the hill. Near the top are large flagstones used to surface the track.

Very little remains of the pathway on the other side of the hill, but the route lies towards a farmhouse at the foot of the hill to the north-east. In good weather the view of Mount Brandon and the land spread out below it is excellent. To the right of the summit of Mount Brandon is Brandon Peak, to the left is Masatiompan; and below is the valley of the Feohanagh River.

To the left of the farmhouse, just above a recently built bungalow, are the remains of the early Christian enclosure of *Cráilí*. Until the turn of the century there was an oratory here, but it was demolished and now only a few stones of the oratory and of three *clocháin* remain. There is a broken cross-slab of about the seventh century with an attractive design, and this was undoubtedly a settlement similar to that at Reask.

The visiting walker may understandably become confused after reading some of the literature about the Saints' Road, because some authors refer to the "Pilgrims' Route" or the "Pilgrims' Path", and some take the "Saints' Road" on routes which have nothing to do with this historic pilgrimage path. This route has nothing to do with the Saints' Road or pilgrims. Some of these diversions from the Saints' Road are undertaken because the route of the Saints' Road leads to the top of Mount Brandon, which is often covered by cloud, and which is not safe to be

recommended as a year-round walk. The route of the Saints' Road pro-
ceeds from *Cráilí* via Ballinloghig and Ballybrack Bridge to Ballybrack,
where it begins its ascent of Mount Brandon.

On the left of Ballybrack Bridge, on the bank of the Feohanagh River,
stands an unusual crescent ringfort. It is in the townland and parish of
Kilquane, *Cill Chúáin*, named after a saint who founded a settlement
here of which no trace remains.

Beyond the bridge a right turn leads to Ballybrack. From the middle
of the village a tarmac road leads up towards the mountain. Its surface
soon becomes stone; it crosses a bridge and continues beside a small
gorge. Stone gives way to a grassy track at a gate, and after passing
through a gap in a wall the route of the Saints' Road turns left and
straight uphill, keeping the nearby stream on the left. Some markers were
privately erected in the '90s, but the route is simple enough, as it goes
straight to the summit without twists or turns. At the summit and any-
where on the eastern face of the mountain great caution is needed; it is
easy to be lulled by the terrain on the western side into ignoring the haz-
ards of the precipitous northern side, which has claimed lives. In particular, it is dangerous to walk around on the summit in the midst of cloud;
no one retains their sense of direction in such circumstances and even
people familiar with the mountain may find themselves heading south-
east for a cliff instead of south-west.

At the summit are the ruins of an early religious settlement: a small oratory, a second rectangular building, a holy well, a cross-inscribed stone
and some mounds, or penitential cairns, which are sometimes referred to
as graves. Surrounding all these are the barely discernible traces of an
enclosure. From the air the enclosure is much clearer and aerial photog-
rapher and author Daphne Pochin Mould has identified what look like
two further walls outside this enclosing bank. This suggests the fascinating possibility that this important Christian site may have been built
inside an existing Iron Age hilltop fort; however, that is only a possibility. Tradition has it that this was a settlement of St Brendan and that it was
from here that he sighted the land of "Hy Brasil", which resolved him on
sailing into the western ocean on his famous voyage.

The ruins have been disturbed, probably on several occasions, over a
period of some fourteen centuries, and by 1756 the oratory was reported

by Smith (*The Antient and Present State of the County of Kerry*) to be in ruins. In 1868 temporary altars were erected and in the process stones were uncovered that seemed to come from a more substantial building than an oratory or *clochán* of the early Christian settlement. The pillar stone is known as *Leac na nDrom*; Fionn Mac Cumhail is said to have backed into it rather sharply while retreating from a large fire in which he was burning some enemies; by some kind of reversal of sympathetic magic the stone was credited with curing backache.

The pilgrimage to the summit was an important one, known for many centuries throughout Ireland and probably in Europe. As Kilmalkedar was the principal religious centre on the peninsula, the most noted part of the pilgrimage was from there to the summit; but pilgrims attended also from the many religious settlements on the peninsula, most of which were concentrated in the western part, close to the route of the Saints' Road, and from further afield. A story which entered the folklore tradition illustrates the popularity of the pilgrimage: the priest presiding at the celebration arrived at the summit at the head of a line of pilgrims only to find that he had left his prayer book behind. Word was passed back down the line, the end of which was still only leaving Kilmalkedar; so the last in the line collected the book from the presbytery and passed it on up the line to the summit.

At the height of Kilmalkedar's importance as a centre of worship and scholarship, the pilgrimage was one of the most important in Ireland and, if Peter Harbison is right, it was the central element of an elaborate and extensive pilgrimage network stretching from the western edge of the old world even as far, perhaps, as the New World.

The church is twelfth century and St Brendan's House is probably fifteenth century, but there is little sign of any real development of the centre of a kind that would suggest that it was particularly important after the twelfth century; probably its prominence belonged basically to the period from the seventh to twelfth centuries. But the pilgrimage remained well known in succeeding centuries. In 1542, for example, a man called Heaneas Mac Haill from Armagh, who had murdered his son, was sent for penance on a tour of the principal pilgrimage sites of the country, one of which was Mount Brandon, and another of which was Skellig Michael. The site at the mountain's summit is named as

Collis Sancti Brendani (the hill of St Brendan) in the Papal Taxation List of 1302–07, and the church here paid a higher tax than any other on the peninsula on account of its high revenue from pilgrims.

In 1868 a revival of the pilgrimage played a part in the triumphant counter-offensive of Roman Catholicism after the Protestants had succeeded in gaining converts. Twenty thousand people are said to have taken part in the pilgrimage in June, some coming by boat from the north and the south.

BRANDON HEAD

Faiche na Manach

MASATIOMPAN

BALLYNAHOW

LOUGH DUFF

BRANDON
CREEK

TIDUFF

St. Brendan's Oratory

Doonroe

Cahers

BALLINKNOCKANE

BALLYDAVID HEAD

Clochán

Signal Tower

GRAFFEE

BALLYCURRANE

Lough

BRANDON
MOUNTAIN

BALLYROE

BALLYNAVENOORAGH EIGHTRAGH

BALLYNABUCK

MOORESTOWN

Cahers

CLASH

Clochán

Saints' Road

FEOHANAGH
An Feothanach

BALLYBRACK

BALLINLOGHIG

LOUGH NAMNA

KILCOOLY

Saints' Road

BALLYDAVID

MURREAGH
An Mhuiríoch

Saints' Road

REENCONNELL

CAHERDARGAN

KILMALKEDAR

GLIN

Castle
Gallarus
Oratory

BALLINRANNIG

BALLYNANA

REASK

EMLAGH

TEMPLENA
CLOONAGH

BALLINEANIG

Gallán
LATEEVEMORE

Saints

KNOCKAVROGEEN

BALLYEABOUGHT

THE NORTH-WESTERN FRONTIER

MASSIVE CLIFFS IN the north-western corner of the peninsula are rocky bulwarks against the power of the Atlantic seas. A roughly triangular area between Murreagh, Ballinloghig and Tiduff can be explored along narrow roads that describe a loop through wild, open landscape between Mount Brandon and the ocean. The coast is encountered intermittently and for part of the route Ballydavid Head rears up between road and sea. Towering cliffs are within easy reach of the walker. One of the most unspoilt, undeveloped parts of the peninsula, its special atmosphere owes much to the fact that no through road passes through it. It is an area with tremendous appeal for the rambler and for the visitor who likes to take things at a leisurely pace. And because it has not, despite its attractiveness, been promoted as a tourist destination within the peninsula, it remains peaceful even through the busy summer months. There are outstanding walks, into Coumaloghig or up to Arraglen, and the evening views out over the last edge of land to the Atlantic can be outstanding.

From Murreagh a road leads to Ballydavid, a small fishing community with two pubs. This is a place to be at sunset and to walk along the coast beyond the village. Many an hour can be whiled away in conversation in the pubs, and with a bit of luck you might arrive one night when music is being played.

The mast in Ballydavid is that of Radio na Gaeltachta, an important institution in the area, which broadcasts in Irish. Established in the wake of agitation by the Gaeltacht civil rights campaign of the 1960s and '70s, it provides programmes of music, documentaries and news. It has done a great deal to raise consciousness of the values, which are too often taken for granted, of the oral tradition of song and story. Its impact goes beyond its broadcast programmes, for it provides production, journalistic and technical employment – jobs of a kind not previously available in the area.

The name of Ballydavid can cause some confusion, because it is also called *Baile na nGall* or Ballynagall, which means in English the townland of the foreigner. It is likely that the foreigners referred to were the Vikings, for Smerwick Harbour was a Viking settlement from which butter was shipped to Limerick. The name Smerwick comes from two Norse words, *smoer* and *wik*, meaning butter and harbour.

Placenames can be confusing, especially for the visitor. In almost all cases the original name is in Irish and has a relatively clear meaning which often conveys something of the history of the place. However, English rule meant that placenames were anglicised to suit the English tongue; often the result is that the name on the map is a mangled version of the real name and hides its meaning. It can also make things difficult for the visitor. Dingle's proper name is *Daingean Uí Chúis* which, to fit on signposts, is generally abbreviated to *An Daingean*, but any foreigner can be forgiven for finding it difficult to match the two forms of the name in Irish with the anglicised version, Dingle.

From Murreagh the main road leads north to Feohanagh through Carrig, Ballylusky and Ardamore. At the junction of the road to Kilcooly is a church and a little further on is *Teach Siamsa*, a large white thatched building which is one of the halls of *Siamsa Tíre*, a folk drama organisation which provides a training for local young people in dance, drama, music and song, as well as giving performances. Visitors should enquire at the Dingle Tourist Office or locally to find out details of any events that may be scheduled.

North of Ardamore are wonderful views of Smerwick Harbour, Ballydavid Head and the beautifully situated pier at Dooneen. In Feohanagh one road leads east while another crosses marshland and the Feohanagh River to continue north and north-east. There is a pub here and a community hall which houses a remarkably lively amateur drama group, *Aisteorí Bhreanainn*, and which plays host to Irish language drama festivals. In nearby Moorestown examples of the traditional currach, or *naomhóg*, are made by Eddie Hutchinson.

The name Feohanagh comes from an old Irish word for a windy place, and when a gale is blowing the wind sweeps with tremendous force across the flatlands. A large, deep bog covered much of the land to the east, and turf from the bog provided the main fuel for the fires of Dingle until the end of the last century. In earlier centuries the area enjoyed a remarkable reputation. Less evidence remains here of early Christian settlements than between Reask and Kilmalkedar, but literary sources suggest that it was a famous monastic centre and even some kind of Garden of Eden. In *Historia Naturas*, published in 1635, John Eusabius Nieramberg wrote:

> In Austral Munster, between Brandon Mountain and the wide sea that washes Spain and Ireland, there is a certain place not altogether limited in extent which is confined on one side by a river abounding in fish, and on the other by some small stream. This place affords an asylum never before heard of, not alone to men and cattle, but also the wild beasts foreign and native. Hence both stags and boars, hares and other animals living in a wild state, when they feel they can nowise escape the dogs following at their heels, betake themselves as

quick as they can – even from parts hence far remote to the same spot
– and as soon as ever they cross the small stream they are at once freed
from all danger by the stoppage of the dogs upon its banks, and their
resistance from further pursuits.

The abundance of potential food in the area was connected in the legend
with the sanctity of the people who had established early settlements here.
As a deterrent to the exploitation of this abundance, anything caught had
to be eaten the same day: by the next day it would have gone bad.

The area north of the Feohanagh River does appear to have possessed
major early Christian sites, but little of them survives. Tradition asserts
that St Brendan's main settlement in the area was here at the foot of
Mount Brandon. Near Ballynavenooragh is Shanakeel, or *Sean-Chill*,
usually translated as "the old church": and at the western foot of
Masatiompan a remarkable site clinging to steep cliffs is called *Faiche na
Manach* or *Fothar na Manaigh*, the green fields of the monks.

The road opposite the pub in Feohanagh is signposted to Brandon
Creek; after crossing the bridge it turns right. A short distance further on
a bohareen leads to the left beside a house with scallop shells on its
gatepost. This is the start of an exhilarating walk along the cliffs to
Brandon Creek. Follow the bohareen until it peters out, then strike
uphill towards the tower. One of a number along the coast, Ballydavid
Tower was built at the beginning of the nineteenth century as a lookout
and signal tower against an expected French invasion. The smaller building was the garrison house. Continuing the walk with its dramatic views
to the north, after about half a mile there is a clifftop path which leads
to Brandon Creek.

Those driving from Feohanagh should continue along the road
through the clusters of houses that make up Ballynabuck, Ballyroe and
Ballycurrane until they reach Brandon Creek.

Brandon Creek, *Cuas an Bhodaigh*, or Coosavuddig, is the place from
which St Brendan is said to have set sail for the "Heavenly Isles" and perhaps for America. In 1977, in asuccessful attempt to establish the
feasibility of such a voyage, a craft made of hides with a crew captained
by Tim Severin set out for North America from Brandon Creek.

The account of the voyage of Brendan, the *Navigatio*, attained enormous fame in medieval Europe and is one of the classic adventure stories

into the village a road continues into the valley of Coumaloghig and becomes a rough track. Waterproof footwear is needed, as on most walks, but an easy stroll along the track brings one deep into the valley and up to the massive headwall of Gearhane. There are signs of tillage on the right and on a spur above stood a spectacularly isolated farmhouse until late in the last century. On the left there are pre-bog field fences on the northern side of the river.

From Ballinloghig the main road to Dingle continues south through a low pass, leaving behind the north-western triangle of the peninsula.

An Bóthar Pub

Muiris & Aileen Walsh, Cuas, 8 miles north from Dingle

Tel: 066 9155342

E-mail: botharpub@eircom.net   Website: www.botharpub.com

- Traditional music, dance and craic • Local arts and crafts
- Bed & Breakfast: ensuite bedrooms; family rooms
- Restaurant and bar food

BRANDON POINT

SAUCE
CREEK

△ SLIEVEGLASS MURIRRIGANE

LISNAKEALWEE

BRANDON BAY

BRANDON

Cé Bhreánainn

△ MASATIOMPAN

MAGHANVEEL

OWENNAFEANA RIVER

BALLYQUIN

LOUGH DUFF

CLOONSHARRAGH

CAPPAGH

FAHA

FERMOYLE

Promontory Fort

CLOGHANE

Gallán

KILCUMMIN

△ MOUNT
BRANDON

LOUGH
NALACKEN

DROM

LOUGH
CRUTTIA

BALLYDUFF

DREHIDGORTANAHA

OWENMORE RIVER

SCORID RIVER

GLENAHOO RIVER

△ BRANDON
PEAK

KILMORE

Gallán
Wedge Grave

LOUGH AVOONANE

CONNOR PASS

LOUGH ADOON
Promontory
Fort △ SLIEVENAGOWER

LOUGH CAMCLAUN

Brandon, Cloghane and Castlegregory

Less affected by the increase in tourism that has occurred in other parts of the peninsula during the last thirty years, the Brandon and Cloghane area is a beautiful haven of serenity. Visitors who want the ready availability of a wide range of musical pubs, of varieties of restaurants and other facilities will tend to stay in or around Dingle town; those with a particular interest in Irish will stay in Ballyferriter and other parts west of Dingle. But for visitors who like the quiet life of walking, of fishing and other outdoor pursuits, and who warm to the charms of sleepy villages with small, cosy pubs and smaller shops, the Brandon-Cloghane area has immense appeal. The entire Dingle peninsula enjoys the close combination of mountains and sea, but nowhere, perhaps, is that relationship closer than at this eastern foot of the highest mountain on the peninsula. Like the area at the western foot of the mountain, the absence of a through road helps lend it a specially attractive quality.

Mount Brandon stands at what was for many centuries the outer edge of the known world. Formed some two hundred million years ago, it is one hundred and seventy million years older than the Himalayas. The millennia of erosion have given its western slopes a gently rounded shape, made softer by the covering of blanket bog; but on the northern side steep cliffs present a high, craggy rampart to the sea, and the eastern face of the mountain falls abruptly to large corries.

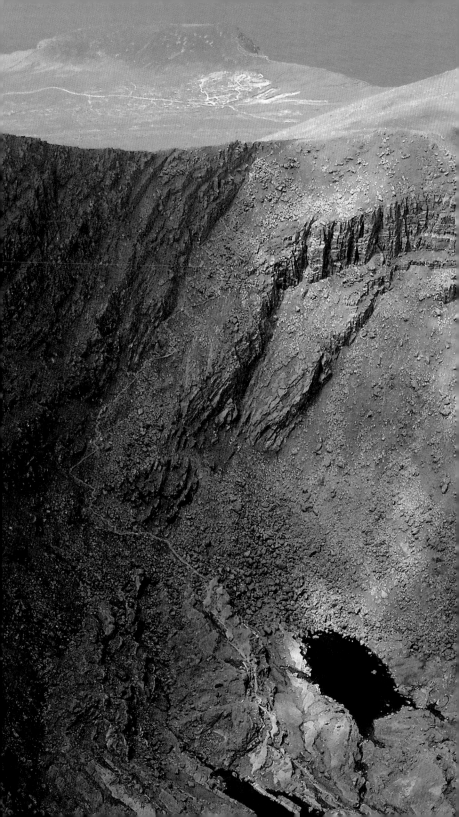

The summit is at a height of 3127 feet (953 metres) and on a clear day offers views as far as the Aran Islands to the north, Dursey Head to the south; and in between, to the east, the cliffs of County Clare, the Shannon estuary, the plains of north Kerry, the mountain ranges (prominent amongst them Carrauntuohill, the only mountain in Ireland higher than Brandon), Dingle Bay and the Iveragh Peninsula. To the west is the vast expanse of the Atlantic, seeming to bear as a burden the ever-changing weather, its waters betraying advancing storms.

By comparison with its physical history, the history of human association with the mountain is no more than a moment. But it is an extraordinarily rich and full moment, offering insight into elements of early civilisation which were once common to all the people of Europe.

We have seen already that a major pilgrimage ascended the south-western side of the mountain, but before the advent of Christianity the mountain was a centre of ritual. In the wall of a ruined thirteenth-century church in Cloghane, at the eastern foot of the mountain, was a pre-Christian carved stone head, and this was, until recently, a vital physical link with the ancient festival, celebrated here, of Lughnasa. Sadly, this very important piece of our heritage was stolen in the 1990s.

High places have been chosen as religious sites throughout the world since the earliest times, and Lughnasa, which was perhaps the most

important Celtic festival, was generally celebrated at hilltop sites. Another name for the festival was *Bron-trogáin*, meaning the bringing forth of the fruits of the earth, and its importance is stressed in an early poem in the *Book of Leinster*, which promises prosperity and abundances of fish, fruit, milk and corn if the festival is celebrated but warns of disaster if it should be ignored.

The central symbol of the festival was the temporary victory of Lug, a bright, young god of many talents, over the older, darker god, Crom Dubh. In dramatic representation of this victory the carved stone head of Crom Dubh was buried at a nearby height. Other aspects of the rites included the sacrifice of a bull and the eating of it, a mythical dance drama, the cutting of the first corn and its presentation to Lug, and general feasting.

Various complex interrelationships of the Celtic gods link Lug with Cú Raoi Mac Daire of Caherconree and also with Cúchulainn, Fionn, Balor, Daire Donn and Goll. In the Celtic pantheon the main figures were the hero and the sun-god, both of which possessed a number of embodiments. Lug, Lugaid, Cúchulainn, Find and Fionn conform to the hero-type, while the sun-god takes the forms of Crom Dubh, Cú Raoi Mac Daire, Daire Donn, Balor and Goll. The degree to which these forms are human or godlike varies considerably, and within the personae there is the ability to take different forms, including those of animals. To confuse the matter further, the pagan gods were often standing stones, as in the story of St Patrick's defeat of Crom Cruach and his twelve attendant stones.

The early Christians attempted to appropriate and "christianise" the pagan ritual, replacing worship of the sun-god with that of Christ, whom they described as "the light of the world". Thus the festivals did not die with the advent of Christianity, and in her outstanding book, *The Festival of Lughnasa*, Máire MacNeill identifies a great number of Lughnasa sites through the length and breadth of Ireland and describes not only their legendary associations but also the semi-parliamentary and other social, political, sporting and cultural aspects of such assemblies.

Some time after the advent of Christianity Lug was replaced in most cases by St Patrick but here, at Mount Brandon, by St Brendan. Crom Dubh retained his place in the legend but was reduced to the status of a local pagan chieftain and converted to Christianity with the assistance of a bull. St Brendan's background was integrated with the pagan legend by the name given to his father: Findlug, a combination of Lug and one of his alternative names, Find.

The traditional form of the Christian *turas* at the mountain was to start out from either Faha in the east or Ballybrack in the west and to climb to the summit, where religious ceremonies would be held, followed by visits to St Brendan's well and the old church in Cloghane. It is in respect of this Cloghane aspect of the pilgrimage that its derivation from pre-Christian festivities seems most evident. Certainly it seems that for many centuries the "pattern" in Cloghane was the most important annual festival on the peninsula, and it is likely that its pagan precursor was every bit as important in the lives of the people of the area before the coming of Christianity.

The eastern side of the mountain is also the location for the most remarkable hilltop promontory fort in Ireland. This fort stands on a peak at 2600 feet (800 metres) due west of the cluster of houses at Faha in the parish of Cloghane; marked on the 6–inch Ordnance Survey map as Benagh, it is known locally as *Binn na Port*. It is a peak which is also a promontory, a knife-edge ridge or *arête* between corries to its north and south, and it is shaped like the prow of a ship. The steep southern and northern cliffs are of exposed rock and jagged with protruding boulders. To the south is the corrie of Coumaknock with its paternoster lakes, to

the north is the corrie of Cumeennagnauv and beyond it the broad expanse of Maghanveal. To the east the line of the promontory continues as a sweeping ridge towards Brandon Bay.

The fort consists of two stone ramparts. The first stands at the point of the mountain where it falls steeply to the south and north and is about 100 metres long. The second, 120 metres west of the first, is 30 metres long, and both run north-south. Built of large and medium sized stones laid horizontally, the better preserved sections of the walls are about 2 metres thick and stand up to 2 metres high. There are entrances in both walls.

It occupies a commanding position 2625 feet (800 metres) high at the western boundary of Lettragh, the area north of the central ridge of the Dingle Peninsula and east of the Brandon range. The walls must once have been a prominent feature of the landscape, for even in their present ruined state they are visible – weather permitting – against the skyline from much of the surrounding countryside. Indeed, from Cloghane it is possible to identify the entrance in the lower wall.

At the eastern extremity of the peninsula stands the similar hilltop promontory fort of Caherconree, and the proximity of these two important monuments strongly suggests that this area was a vital and powerful centre of activity in the Iron Age. About fifty hill-forts have been identified in Ireland, of which only two others, in County Antrim, are of the same kind – inland promontory forts – as Caherconree and Benagh.

Defining hill-forts, Barry Raferty ("Irish Hill-Forts" in *The Iron Age in the Irish Sea Province*; C.B.A. Research Report 9: 1972) has written:

In Ireland these monuments are seen to be extensive areas of land within one or more ramparts of earth or stone, defending, it must be assumed, rather than merely enclosing a hilltop or other strongly defensible natural position. The size, situation and magnitude of the defences of the hill-forts must denote centres of tribal rather than of family significance. In most cases the hill-fort may be regarded as having had, primarily, a defensive function, though in some exceptional cases religious importance or significance as places of inauguration or assembly may have contributed paramount distinction. The exact uses to which the enclosed area was put is a matter of conjecture.

The function and significance of Benagh had more to do with religion, inauguration or assembly than with practical defence, and it is likely that this was the hilltop site of the festival of Lughnasa. Another function of the fort was probably display; when the walls stood to their full height they would have been visible from far and wide in the surrounding countryside and from the sea. Benagh in this way was a symbol of confidence and power – the power of the tribe and of their gods.

FROM FAHA, where the mountain pathway starts, the surfaced road passes through Ballynalacken to Cloonsharragh. Here, up *an bóthar dorcha*, the dark road, there is a very fine alignment of three standing stones.

A string of small communities lies in a line to the north on the edge of Brandon Bay. On a point jutting into the bay just east of Ballyquin is a caher, or stone fort, some 120 feet (36.5 metres) across. There is a fine beach here, which is red from the coastal erosion of old red sandstone, but it is not safe for bathing.

The pier at Brandon village is quiet enough these days, but a century ago as many as a hundred canoes used to fish from here, in addition to several larger craft, bringing in mackerel which were cured on the quays by women and children. The salted mackerel were sent in large quantities to North America, but it was a trade which suffered a sudden and complete decline. From Brandon, too, butter was sent to Cork by sea and by pack horse. The old pier and coastguard station were built in 1825 and the present pier in 1896.

Nearby Lisnakealwee boasts an early song in celebration of Gaelic football. Like many such songs, its major objective seems to be to mention the names of as many people as possible – a function to be compared with the arrays of photographs in today's local newspapers. It also features a woman goalkeeper, and a few verses give an idea of the characteristic virtues of the local song tradition:

They had men from all quarters from hills and from dale,
They had young Mike O'Donnell and likewise Andy Kane:
It was safer for them to stay herding their sheep
Than to face the bold boys of Lios na Caol Bhuidhe.

There was a blacksmith from Camp there, they called him Tom Crean.
Like Carroll he wanted to make a cat of two tails,

Before half time was over he had to retreat
And get sticking plaster to screw on his teeth.

As in other countries, sport in Ireland engages the energies of many young people and enjoys fierce local support, and throughout County Kerry the sport of sports is Gaelic football. A particular factor in Ireland is that the Gaelic Athletic Association was formed as part of a general development of cultural and political nationalism in the late nineteenth century, and to this day there is a GAA ethos which goes beyond the practical business of organising the sports. Visitors wishing to attend a Gaelic football match will usually be able to find out about fixtures in the nearest pub.

Murririgane was once the home of the leading family of the Brandon Bay area, the Geraldine sept of *Sliocht* (kin of) Edmund. By the eighteenth century these Fitzgeralds were smugglers reduced to the economic and social level of their neighbours; but in the sixteenth century they had possessed castles at Fermoyle and Cloghane and had been the effective local overlords. Their fortunes tumbled with the fall of Desmond, on whose side they had fought, and in 1583 their lands passed to Sir Walter Raleigh and others, thence to the Earl of Cork, whose tenants they became.

Brandon Point is a fine place for the birdwatcher, and many evenings offer the sight of Manx shearwaters at the Head. Off here, too, are good lobster beds.

Although the number of canoes and boats using the bay has declined to very few now, there is still an annual regatta. The bay can be dangerous as it is affected both by winds from off the mountains and by being so open to the sea, and a number of ships and boats have been wrecked here over the years.

In November 1965 sixty-three pilot whales stranded themselves on the beach at Cloghane; and on the pattern day in July 1918 a school of porpoise also became stranded.

Brandon Point is known in Irish as *Srub Brain*, and it was here that Bran and his crew came after sailing in the heavenly western isles and spending what they thought was only a year on the Island of Women. Of course, they had been away much longer, and when one of their number set foot on shore at *Srub Brain* he turned at once to a pile of dust.

The area between Brandon Bay and Masatiompan, apart from the narrow coastal strip with its cluster of houses, is an eerie moorland wilderness bounded to the north by massive cliffs. The experienced hill walker will find it interesting – such landscape is, after all, very rare – but the casual countryside stroller might be better advised to stick to less tiring ground. The most dramatic coastal feature is Sauce Creek, a large U-shaped inlet with high, steep scree-strewn slopes. The name may seem strange, but as is so often the case the anglicisation has made nonsense of it. The Irish word *sás* means a trap of a kind using a noose, and in this case describes the action of the sea within the creek: as a fisherman remarked, "Anything that goes in there won't come out no more."

It is extraordinary to think, looking at the creek, that three families lived there in the last century, and that one of those families remained into the early years of this century. But above Sauce to the east and west lived more families on what seems equally inhospitable land. At Slieve Glass lived fourteen families in the eighteenth century, though none remained there by the mid-nineteenth. And to Arraglen, half a mile west of Sauce, came thirteen families who had fought with their neighbours at *Baobh an Chnoic*, Murririgane; ruins of some of the houses, one of which is in relatively good condition, may still be seen. Here they grew wheat and rye and kept livestock; and in the evening light cultivation ridges are still visible beneath the heather.

Cloghane is the main focus of this peaceful and beautiful corner of the peninsula. Until early this century the pattern on *Domhnach Crom Dubh*, the last Sunday in July, remained the most important day in the local calendar. Emigrants to America, Europe and Britain used to time their visits home to coincide with the festival. People bought new clothes or made them; they painted and cleaned their homes and prepared food. "Pattern pies" were made and sold; fiddlers came and played for their pennies; tinkers converged with their wares; and there were games and dancing and entertainments from the afternoon until early next morning. On the Monday there was a special dance in Brandon.

To the east of Cloghane the small hill is called Drom and near a track here are four *galláin*, one of which is partly hidden. At Fermoyle, near by, the two large houses belonged to two branches of the Hickson family, prominent local landowners who came to the peninsula in the seventeenth century and married into the Husseys of Dingle.

TO CLIMB Mount Brandon take the road north from Cloghane and the first left off it, then turn left again and continue to the end of the road at Faha. Here there is a notice bearing warnings about precautions that must be taken, and from here a pathway leads to the mountain summit. Near by is a pleasantly laid out and well maintained grotto; the ridge above it

can be seen to sweep up to the west, and on a clear day one can see where it comes to a peak: this peak is Benagh, and walkers who wish to visit it should detour from the pathway before it swings to the left below.

After curving left with the shape of the hill the path swings right, into a spectacular glaciated valley strung with paternoster lakes. The larger lakes below are Lough Nalacken – *Loch na Leacan*, hillside lake and Lough Cruttia – *Loch Croichte*, hanging lake. The fine peak above to the south is Brandon Peak, which is distinct from the summit but which, by virtue of its shape, often seems to be higher than it.

Rock layers curve in the dark mass of mountain headwall. To the untrained eye the dark rock would hardly seem the place for notable plant growth, but on ledges in the highest reaches of the valley grow the rarest flora on the peninsula – the arctic alpine flora which survived only above the line of Ice Age glaciation. It is a rewarding site for botanists: although each of the plants occurs in one or two other places in Ireland, only here does one find them close to each other.

The final part of this path twists steeply up a cliff of about 700 feet; it should be approached with caution and is not for the faint-hearted. Once at the top of the cliff, turn south along the ridge to the summit and St Brendan's oratory.

THE AREA south of Fermoyle and up to the Connor Pass is well worth visiting for a number of features, in particular for the fine examples of corries. Just a few miles south of Cloghane are the corrie lakes of Lough Adoon, Lough Camclaun and Lough Doon, which lies close to the Connor Pass. In few places is the effect of ice action as clearly shown as in these corries and cirques. Indeed, it was at Lough Doon that an important breakthrough in understanding glaciation was made when, in 1849, the Alpine mountaineer, John Ball, recognised that this corrie was of the same type as others in Switzerland.

The popular name for Lough Doon is Pedlar's Lake; and there is, of course, a story behind this. It is told in several different versions, but this is how I first heard it. A young man from Anascaul was returning home after travelling the world; dressed as a pedlar, he fell in with two thieves who robbed and killed him, throwing him into the lake. Later, in Anascaul they were showing off their ill-gotten gains when the man's lover whom he had left behind recognised a broken sixpence she had given him as a token. So, Pedlar's Lake it is known as; but why it should have been called Lough Doon remains tantalisingly uncertain. A possible – indeed, most likely – explanation is that there was a *dún* or promontory fort on the *arête* above the lake on its eastern side. Close by the Connor Pass road, this is the most accessible of the corrie lakes, its shape a reminder that the Irish word *coire* means cauldron. There is a place directly below it where cars can pull in.

Both Lough Camclaun and Lough Adoon can also be approached from the road across the blanket bog. Between these two lakes stands Slievenalecka: appropriately known as "the steeple", it is in geological terms a horn, formed, like an *arête*, by the wearing away by ice action of the corries on three sides. Lough Adoon is named after an unusual fort, which takes the form of a wall across an island. The lake is shallow enough for one to walk across to the island.

An extensive series of neolithic and Early Bronze Age remains which pre-date the formation of the blanket bog lies on either side of the Scorid River at Ballyhoneen, below Lough Adoon. To the west of the river is a large network of pre-bog walls which once surrounded the fields of the first farmers who settled in this area in the neolithic period. Their existence has been revealed by a combination of turf-cutting and erosion; some are almost completely exposed, some are still partly covered by peat,

and others presumably still lie unexposed under uncut sections of the bog here. In the north-western sector of the pre-bog field system is a large boulder decorated with cup-and-circle rock art, which is probably of the Early Bronze Age. Also on the western side of the river are the sites of several dry-stone huts, but the principal structures lie on the eastern side.

A wedge-tomb stands on a low hillock about 574 feet (175 metres) east of the river, partly buried in the bog, its base filled with water. Three of the stones of the tomb are decorated with rock art. About 213 feet (65 metres) north of it is a standing stone and 279 (85 metres) further north another one. South-west of the tomb are the ruins of two dry-stone huts. Two *fulacht fiadh* sites lie north of the standing stones. One is on the eastern bank of the river, which has eroded it, while a holly tree has also disturbed this site. But the fragments of burnt stone, the black soil and the horseshoe-shaped mound are typical of this kind of site. The other *fulacht fiadh* here in Ballyhoneen lies about 574 feet (175 metres) to the north-east.

Taken as a whole, the Ballyhoneen area must be regarded as one of the prime archaeological sites on the peninsula, and it is quite likely that we will learn more about it during the next few years. In places such as this the pre-bog landscape has been quite well preserved, along with the field systems, settlements and graves of the early farmers. The development of blanket bog is thought to have begun by the late 3rd millennium BC, and it continued to develop in new areas as late as the twelfth century AD. The walls that are preserved beneath the bogs are not necessarily neolithic, though some such field systems have been definitely dated to that period, and a pre-bog wall in County Kerry, on Valentia Island, has been dated to before 2650 BC. At sites such as Ballyhoneen, the fact that rock art, wedge-tombs and standing stones are found within the ancient field systems suggests quite strongly an Early Bronze Age date.

Where the Connor Pass road is met by the Cloghane Road is Kilmore Lodge, from which an infamous road was built to the pass in 1759. Like many of the roads conceived by landlords in this period, it was impractically built, with a final section of one-in-three gradient zig-zagging as it struggled to the top. Where its dead-straight course rises beside the present road – built in the 1830s – there are ruined houses and *clocháin* beside it.

There is a sharp bend at Drehidgortanaha, and the next turn south leads into Glennahoo and towards Maghanaboe. The bohareen quickly peters out, but the dramatically sculpted valley invites the walker, and it is possible, if one has several hours to spend, to walk over to Anascaul by the old track. Just north-east of Maghanaboe are four substantial peaks, the highest of which is Beenoskee. Deep inside the Glennahoo Valley lived two families, the Dineens and the O'Donnells, who were shepherds for Conway Hickson, looking after a large number of sheep at Maghanaboe. Hickson, a substantial landowner from Fermoyle, was an improving landlord who organised the attempted drainage of the top of Maghanaboe, evidence of which can still be seen.

The shepherds were paid very little and much of what they did receive was in kind, such as wool for making stockings. When Hickson sold up, the Land Commission took over his land and part of it in Glennahoo and Maghanaboe was given to the O'Donnells and the Dineens.

Mary O'Donnell, who lived there with her sister after the Dineens had left, is still well remembered locally, and she became known as "Mary Maghanaboe". One woman in Ballynacourty near Anascaul recalled trekking over the mountains to go to a dance in Stradbally as a young girl. She and her friend wandered off the route of the old track that leads up from behind Anascaul lake and over via Maghanaboe, and as they

approached Maghanaboe the old woman was outside her house yelling at them. It was said that the isolation made her rather odd. Men who had sheep on the mountains also recalled her habit of shouting at them from the doorway of her house. While they were perhaps a little wary of her they used sometimes to call to her house when they were over that way after sheep, for it would be rude to pass by without stopping. She was undoubtedly poor, but she would always give them a cup of tea and a cut of bread with her own butter all the same. At fairs from Anascaul to Castlegregory she cut a striking figure with her long plait of white hair.

STRADBALLY'S HOUSES cluster around the present road, but the old church is near the shore where the old cart road came inland from the beach and turned towards Killiney. There are two churches at Killiney; the fifteenth-century church of Saint Enna and the Protestant church built in 1812. In the churchyard is a 9-foot high stone cross of the eighth or ninth century and a small cross with one arm missing which is probably about a century earlier. There is also a memorial to those drowned in the wreck of the barque *Portyarrock* of Glasgow, which went down in the bay on 29 January 1894 after sailing from Santa Rosalia. Seven bodies were recovered at Killiney, five at Stradbally, and one at Brandon. Part of the wreck can still be seen off the strand at Kilcummin at low tide.

Tobar Éinne lies north of Killiney churchyard and rounds were still made somewhat infrequently here until recent years early in the mornings in May and June, and especially on 24 June. It was once the site of an energetic pattern on 15 August, but this moved into nearby Castlegregory. Following hard on the heels of the Cloghane pattern, it boasted most of the same attractions. An unusual feature was that only men used to take part on 15 August, and women on the following day, known as "Sheila's Day".

Castlegregory is the capital of Lettragh, the northern side of the peninsula; its population is little more than a quarter of what it was shortly before the Famine; but it remains the only place of the area that possess the unity and proportion of a real village.

The castle from which the name comes was built in the mid-sixteenth century by Gregory Hoare, but it is no longer standing. There has long been a tradition that the name derived from the late sixth century Pope,

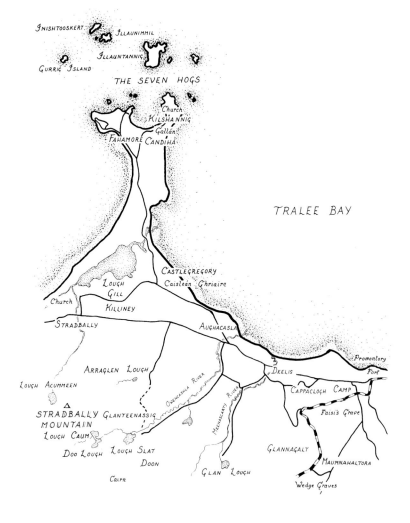

INISHTOOSKERT

ILLAUNIMMIL

ILLAUNTANNIG

GURRIG ISLAND

THE SEVEN HOGS

Church
KILSHANNIG
Gallán
FAHAMORE CANDIHA

TRALEE BAY

CASTLEGREGORY
Caislean Ghriaire

LOUGH GILL

Church
KILLINEY

STRADBALLY

AUGHACASLA

ARRAGLEN LOUGH

Promontory
Fort

DEELIS

LOUGH ACUMMEEN

CAPPACLOGH CAMP

△
STRADBALLY GLANTEENASSIG
MOUNTAIN
LOUGH CAUM

Faisi's Grave

DOO LOUGH LOUGH SLAT
DOON

GLANNAGALT

MAUMNAHALTORA

Cairn

GLAN LOUGH

Wedge Graves

Owencashla River

Meenabasty River

St Gregory the Great, known as Gregory Goldenmouth and claimed to be of the *Corca Dhuibhne* people. However, Pope Gregory was probably confused with another St Gregory who was Irish and associated with the Iveragh Peninsula; Gregory Hoare is the much more likely source of the placename.

There is a story associated with the castle which is reminiscent of the relationship between the Montagues and Capulets in Shakespeare's *Romeo and Juliet*. Gregory Hoare had a feud with a neighbour called Moore. In the face of parental fury Hugh, Gregory's son, married Moore's daughter Ellen in 1566. As they returned to the castle from the wedding Gregory stood at the gate, but his son pushed past him and the unfortunate Gregory fell dead on the spot.

In 1580 part of Lord Grey of Wilton's army – including, it is said, Edmund Spenser, Walter Raleigh and Edward Denny – stayed at the castle on their way to besiege *Dún an Óir*. Outraged at her husband, entertaining the enemy, Hoare's wife, Ellen, went to the cellar and ran off all the wine from the barrels there. Hugh Hoare attacked her and stabbed her to death. Next morning he was summoned to appear before his overlords to answer a charge of murder, but he fell dead as he passed the very place where his father had died fourteen years earlier.

A later marriage, of "Black" Hugh's daughter, transferred the castle to Walter Hussey of Dingle. He supported the Knight of Kerry in the Cromwellian wars and was pursued by Wilmot's forces from Castlegregory to Minard across the mountains. He died in the destruction of Minard Castle and the Husseys were ruined. The castle – "slighted" by the English army – and the estate at Castlegregory were settled first on a Cromwellian soldier, then passed to a Derry man who settled locally, and were bought by the first Lord Ventry in whose family they remained until 1913.

Lough Gill, near Castlegregory, is an important centre for wildfowl, featuring especially the gadwall. It is one of the few places where Bewick's, mute and whooper swans can all be seen. In 1980 the last of the greylag geese on the peninsula appeared to have been adopted by the swans and could be seen flying with a group of them around the lough and south to the mountain coums. The lake is also of considerable significance as a major breeding ground of the rare natterjack toad.

To the north is the spit dividing Tralee and Brandon Bays. The northern tip and the Magharee Islands are surviving outcrops of carboniferous limestone. In the sandy soil of the spit onions, carrots and potatoes grow particularly well, as do daffodils, irises and anemones; and this has been the basis of one of the most thriving modern developments on the peninsula. Distribution and marketing of the produce is carried out by the St Brendan's Co-operative, founded in 1955, and an outward sign of prosperity is the number of new houses to be seen.

The Trench Bridge maintains the level of Lough Gill which drains through sand banks deposited by the sea. Marram grass is extensively planted, and some pine trees, to combat the effects of sea and wind. Near Lough Naparka old houses have disappeared beneath the sand.

There is a particularly large *gallán* – about 14 feet above the ground – at Candiha, standing near the road amidst vegetables. Kilshannig boasts a much later development of the standing stone – a cross-slab of the seventh century with an interestingly designed cross. In common with slabs at Kilfountain and Knockane, the Kilshannig cross includes a representation of *chi-rho* – the Greek initials for Christ – and in this case it is a cryptically formalised loop out of the top of a Latin cross. There is a pagan-derived divergent spiral at the base of the cross. The church here may date in part to the twelfth century but it is mostly a fifteenth to sixteenth century reconstruction. Near the church is the surfboarding school of Jamie Knox, which attracts many visitors in the summer months.

Above the present beach at Fahamore is a raised beach in the cliff behind the old sea wall. Scraggane pier, Fahamore, built in 1887, is one of the last places where the *naomhóg* is still made. Canvas covered by tar was introduced as a substitute for animal skin by a family of Hartneys from Clare who settled here in the 1830s. Races with these specially constructed canoes are held at the Maharees Regatta in June. In the past there was a minor industry in cockles, which were picked, shelled and boiled here and sold to merchants in Tralee; but now there is fishing for mackerel, herring, lobsters, oysters, crayfish and crabs.

For those interested in the early Christian settlements it is especially worthwhile to try to persuade someone to take them over to Illauntannig – *Oileán tSeanaig*. The best thing to do is simply to enquire locally; on a day-long trip around the islands I was cheerfully and well looked after for a very reasonable price. The early settlement of *Seanach* is one of the finest of its kind. The enclosing wall, or cashel, is exceptionally strong – about 18 feet thick – though part of it has fallen to the erosion of the sea. In the larger of the two ruined oratories there is an altar and the

window survives; there are *clocháin*, from one of which a souterrain runs to a chamber in the enclosure wall. There are cross-slabs; and particularly prominent features are three quartz-covered "*leachts*", rectangular burial platforms. By the shore, a hundred yards from the cashel, is a *bullán* with an incised cross. A two-storey farmhouse on the island was occupied until the 1950s; and it is known locally as Learie's Island after the people who lived there.

Inishtooskert, the most north-westerly of the Magharees, was the rendezvous on the night of Holy Thursday in 1916 when the *Aud* waited in vain for a signal from land.

The *Aud* was a German arms ship disguised as a Norwegian freighter and she was carrying 20,000 rifles, 10 machine guns and ammunition, which were intended for the Irish Republican Brotherhood (IRB). It had been arranged that the *Aud* would land the arms at Fenit, at the north of Tralee Bay, between 20 and 23 April; however, owing to a failure in communications, the republicans were expecting the ship on the 23rd – Easter Sunday.

On 20 April, having penetrated the British naval blockade, the *Aud* arrived at the rendezvous off the Maharees island of Inishtooskert. Here it was due to meet at midnight a German U-19 submarine carrying three members of the IRB – Casement, Monteith and Bailey. It was also due to rendezvous with the pilot in Fenit. However, almost everything that could go wrong did go wrong.

The submarine and the *Aud* failed to make contact; the *Aud* was anchored off Castlegregory, several miles from Inishtooskert where the submarine sought it out. After exploring the bay for a while, the submarine crossed to a point two miles off Banna Strand. Casement, Monteith and Bailey landed by dinghy on the strand between Fenit and Ballyheigue. Casement, who was ill, was left at McKenna's ringfort, near Ardfert, while Monteith and Bailey went in to Tralee to seek out Austin Stack, the senior IRB man in the area. After some delay Bailey accompanied Stack in a car to collect Casement, only to find that he had been arrested. Later that day they, too, were arrested.

Meanwhile, the *Aud* was still in Tralee Bay. The pilot in Fenit had been told to watch for a ship showing green lights on the night of 23 April; on the 20th he saw what he took to be blue lights and had no particular reason to think that these were the lights of the *Aud*, which because of the proximity of British naval patrols left the bay for the open sea on the afternoon of Good Friday, 21 April. That evening the ship was captured by the British and the next morning was scuttled with its guns in Cork Harbour.

It had been planned that what had been announced as "manoeuvres" by the republican Volunteers on Easter Sunday would accomplish the distribution of the arms and launch a national rising. However, when on Saturday it became clear that the arms would not be landed, Eoin Mac Neill, one of the leaders of the Volunteers, issued an order cancelling the "manoeuvres".

Monteith, who had been on the submarine with Casement and Bailey, was – in the absence of Austin Stack – in command of 320 Volunteers who assembled in Tralee on Easter Sunday. Amongst them were men who had marched into Tralee from Ballyferriter. In the face of Mac Neill's countermanding order, the Volunteers paraded briefly and dispersed.

What took place the following day in Dublin has since become known as "The Easter Rising" or the "1916 Rising". A small proportion of the Volunteers, together with the Irish Citizen Army under the leadership of the revolutionary socialist, James Connolly, launched an insurrection which was almost entirely confined to Dublin.

Sir Roger Casement, who had served with such distinction in the British colonial service but who had joined the Irish National Volunteers in 1913, was taken from Tralee to stand trial for British "treason" in London, where he was found guilty and hanged. The attempt to bring the arms was an important incident in 1916 and is one of the great "might-have-beens" of the Rising; but while the number of guns could have made a significant difference, the difficulties that would have been encountered in distributing them would have been considerable and probably would not have resulted in the kind of fully effective national mobilisation that was envisaged.

SOUTH OF Castlegregory are mountains and valleys. Glanteenassig – *Gleannta an Easig*, the valleys of the waterfall, has a substantial forestry development and is one of the most beautiful places on the peninsula on a fine day. It is possible to drive right into the deep valley, which resembles the scenery of Killarney and of County Wicklow more than that of

the rest of the peninsula. Peaks and corrie cliffs rise steeply from lakes, and the river meanders, forming oxbow bends, through a long valley which is by turns bleak and rocky, brown and green with planted trees. Deep in the valley a house stands at a bend in the road; walkers can take the well-built stony track which winds up the hill of Doon from beside the house. This track continues as far as a turf-cutting area, but an earlier track swings south-west to a low point on the shoulder south of the mountain ridge where it then drops down into Ballynahunt, near Anascaul. According to some accounts it was by this route that the Cromwellian forces crossed the mountains from Castlegregory to Minard Castle, though others favour the route by Maghanaboe; but for the walker who likes to get up into the hills it is simply an excellent route to take across the mountains.

Lough Slat, Doon Lough and Lough Caum, which attract local anglers, possess a sense of calm amidst the power of massive corrie head-walls. Much of the surrounding forest is pine, but there are other trees and shrubs, especially holly, a characteristic of what was oak forest before the seventeenth century, by which time the forests had been cut down to provide timber for building the British navy and to an extent also for fuel for industry.

The main road between Castlegregory and Camp was the scene during the course of the late nineteenth century land war of many attacks on landlords' agents, bailiffs and process-servers. Later, in 1919, on the same road at Deelis, one of the first ambushes of the War of Independence took place. It is celebrated in a song composed by local man, Michael Mansell, which was sung to me by John Joe Gleeson of Meenascarty; the title of the song is "Barney Oates", after the sargeant of the Royal Irish Constabulary disarmed in the ambush. It opens

> The twenty-fourth day of June in the year 1919
> Some daring young chappoes that night could be seen:
> They brought the gun, the revolver, all ready for fight,
> They had Barney and Connell in Deelis that night.

At Cappaclogh, just before Camp, a road leads to the right to a remarkable valley known as *Gleann na nGealt*, the valley of the mad. Its name and its reputation span the centuries, for it is mentioned in the account

of the Battle of Ventry as the place to which the King of France flew over
the mountains when he lost his wits in the course of the fighting. There
are several instances of elements of the history and folklore of the peninsula becoming known and written about widely in Europe; the strong
reputation of the Feohanagh area at the foot of Mount Brandon is a case
in point. *Gleann na nGealt's* reputation was sufficient in the seventeenth
century for it to be prominently if somewhat facetiously featured in the
account of County Kerry in William Camden's *Britannia* (1695 edition).

> Perhaps some will impute it to want of gravity and prudence in me,
> if I give an account of an old opinion of the wild Irish, and still
> current among them. That he, who in the great clamor and outcry
> (which the soldiers usually make with much straining before an
> onset) does not *Huzza* as the rest do, is suddenly snatch'd from the
> ground, and carried flying into these desert vallies, from any part of
> Ireland whatsoever; that there he eats grass, laps water, has no sense
> of happiness nor misery, has some remains of his reason, but none
> of his speech, and that at long run he shall be caught by the hunters,
> and brought back to his own home.

As late as the nineteenth century people still came from various parts
of Ireland to this valley in pursuit of a cure for madness. Some, it seems,
wandered naked in the valley, and all drank water from the well and
dined on the cresses that grew there. It has been said that the power or
luck of the well left it when two young men from Dublin carried water
away from it in bottles in the early years of this century.

Few people now believe or even remember the superstitions and stories
that once embroidered the cloth of the countryside. They survived late on
this peninsula because of its isolation from economic development; in a
world without television, in a society of subsistence farmers and fishermen, these beliefs and stories were a communal resource of some rich-
ness. They faded in the face of the alternative attractions of the modern
world, and in the accounts of old people it is notable that the period after
World War I is seen as a turning point. This may seem strange, as Ireland
was not involved as a nation in the war, but very large numbers of young
Irishmen fought and died in the British army then, and the horror of
modern warfare filtered its tales back with the wounded. But also the

immediate post-war period saw the War of Independence, followed by the Civil War, both of which were characterised by cruel violence as Ireland dragged itself to the brink of nationhood. It was perhaps a harsh practical reality, allied with the continued depopulation of the area by emigration, that caused the withering away of the oral tradition. Whatever the reason, one old woman told me that "the fairies went from us in 1920".

Television dealt the death-blow to storytelling and the composition of songs. But there is a quality in the speech and conversation of people on the peninsula which inherits something from the store of legends and stories. Not easy to define, it is nevertheless something that registers with many visitors who are able to spend time in the area in the company of local people. Most marked in those for whom Irish is the first language, it is also present in the use of English.

After visitors have taken in the scenery of the peninsula, walked in its hills and visited some of its archaeological sites, the visual memories may be the strongest, but no place is simply the sum of its physical appearance and there is a real sense in which the cliché is true that it is the people that make the place.

THE DINGLE WAY

THE DINGLE PENINSULA is a kind of paradise for the walker. Old roads and pathways free of traffic reach into the heart of a landscape dominated by mountains and hills, sea and cliffs. Many of these routes are bordered by lush hedgerows in which the red-flowered fuchsia predominates, and many of them pass only yards from the historical and archaeological sites for which the peninsula is renowned.

The Dingle Way starts in Tralee, makes its way to the southern coastline of the peninsula, and continues to the western coastline; it turns north along the rocky western cliffs and turns then back east along the northern coastline. It extends for some 112 miles (178 kilometres) in all and passes through Camp, Anascaul, Lispole, Dingle, Ventry, Dunquin, Ballydavid, Cloghane and Castlegregory.

The Pilgrims' Route starts in Dingle, turns south in Ventry, then north; from Reask it turns south again to join the Saints' Road at Lateevebeg; it follows the Saints' Road north through Kilmalkedar as far as Currauley (*Cráilí*), after which it leaves the Saints' Road again and goes by green track and minor road to Cloghane. Passing many sites between Ventry and Currauley which are associated with the early flowering of Christianity in the area, it extends for some 30 miles (48 kilometres). Unfortunately, some confusion has been caused by the fact that "The Pilgrims' Route" is sometimes erroneously called "The Saints' Road". The historic Saints' Road, which is a monument of some considerable national and international significance, extended from Lateevebeg to the summit of Mount Brandon; it is possible that it may also have extended south-westwards from Lateevebeg to Glanfahan, and one might also consider the pilgrimage path from Cloghane to the top of Mount Brandon as being an eastern extension of the Saints'

Road. (The Dingle Way map is unfortunately mistaken in marking the site of the Saints' Road as running over the hill between Maumanorig and Lateeve; as is clear from the 1841/42 and 1896 Ordnance Survey maps, the Saints' Road continued to Lateevebeg.)

The route of the Dingle Way is discreetly marked by posts bearing yellow arrows and/or the symbol of a person walking. Good boots are essential on most sections of the route in most weather. Even in summer some parts of the way may be wet and muddy, while others are dry and stony. The weather can change suddenly and dramatically, so walkers should always carry rain- and wind-proof clothing, together with food, map and whistle. Between Tiduff and Brandon fog or low cloud can cause walkers to lose their way, so those who are not experienced in map reading and navigating may be best advised to avoid this section. In the event of an accident, help can be obtained by dialling 999 and asking for the appropriate service – Mountain Rescue, ambulance, etc.

The Dingle Way and the Pilgrims' Route have been set up with the agreement of local farmers and landowners, and short sections may be diverted from time to time to comply with the needs of landowners. Users should help to preserve goodwill by remembering that the fields are the farmers' workshops, so care must be taken not to damage fences, crops, stock or property. Gates should always be closed after use, and dogs should never be brought on the walk; litter should not be left in fields or on the road or track. Neither route is suitable for bicycles or horses.

It is easy to arrange accommodation close to the Dingle Way: simply obtain from a tourist office a copy of a Bord Fáilte/Irish Tourist Board leaflet called *Long Distance Walking Routes Accommodation*, which lists hotels, guesthouses, town and country homes, farmhouses, caravan and camping parks, and hostels.

Walking the Dingle Way in easy stages

Tralee → Camp	11 miles	17.5 km
Camp → Anascaul	10.5 miles	17 km
Anascaul → Dingle	12 miles	19 km
Dingle → Dunquin	14 miles	22 km
Dunquin → Ballydavid (*Baile na nGall*)	13 miles	21 km
Ballydavid → Cloghane	17.5 miles	28 km
Cloghane → Castlegregory	18 miles	29 km
Castlegregory → Tralee	16 miles	25 km

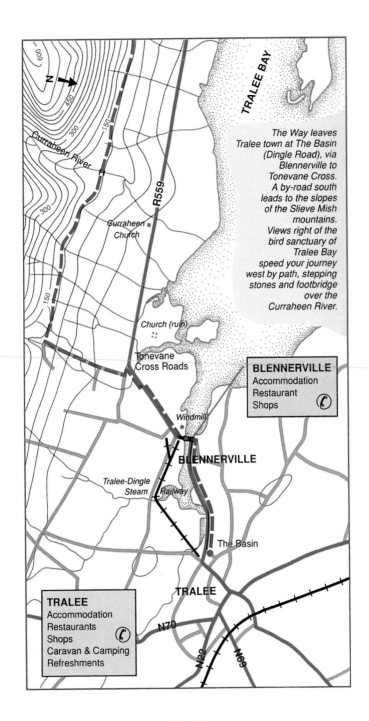

The Way leaves Tralee town at The Basin (Dingle Road), via Blennerville to Tonevane Cross. A by-road south leads to the slopes of the Slieve Mish mountains. Views right of the bird sanctuary of Tralee Bay speed your journey west by path, stepping stones and footbridge over the Curraheen River.

TRALEE BAY

Curraheen River

R559

Curraheen Church

Church (ruin)

Tonevane Cross Roads

Windmill

BLENNERVILLE

Tralee-Dingle Steam Railway

The Basin

BLENNERVILLE
Accommodation
Restaurant
Shops

TRALEE

TRALEE
Accommodation
Restaurants
Shops
Caravan & Camping
Refreshments

N70

N22

N69

Map 1

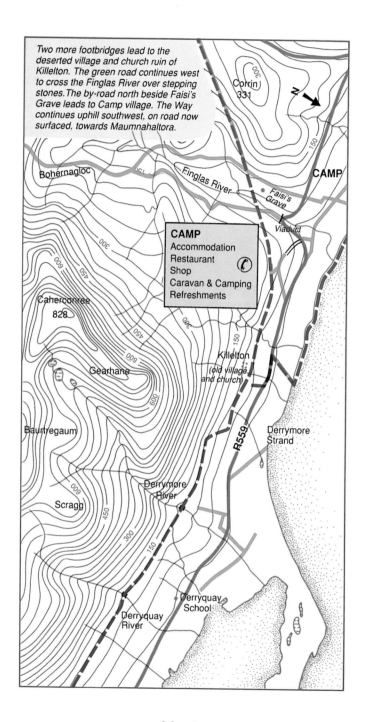

Two more footbridges lead to the deserted village and church ruin of Killelton. The green road continues west to cross the Finglas River over stepping stones. The by-road north beside Faisi's Grave leads to Camp village. The Way continues uphill southwest, on road now surfaced, towards Maumnahaltora.

Corrin 331

Bohernagloc

Finglas River

CAMP

Faisi's Grave

Viaduct

CAMP
Accommodation
Restaurant
Shop
Caravan & Camping
Refreshments

Caherconree 828

Killelton
(old village and church)

Gearhane

Baunregaum

Derrymore Strand

R559

Derrymore River

Scragg

Derryquay School

Derryquay River

Map 2

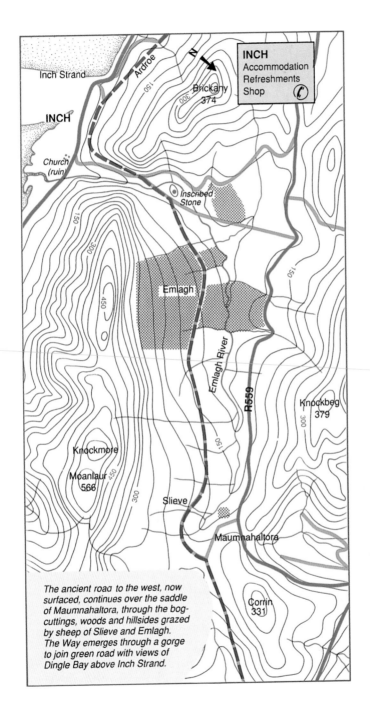

The ancient road to the west, now surfaced, continues over the saddle of Maumnahaltora, through the bog-cuttings, woods and hillsides grazed by sheep of Slieve and Emlagh. The Way emerges through a gorge to join green road with views of Dingle Bay above Inch Strand.

Map 3

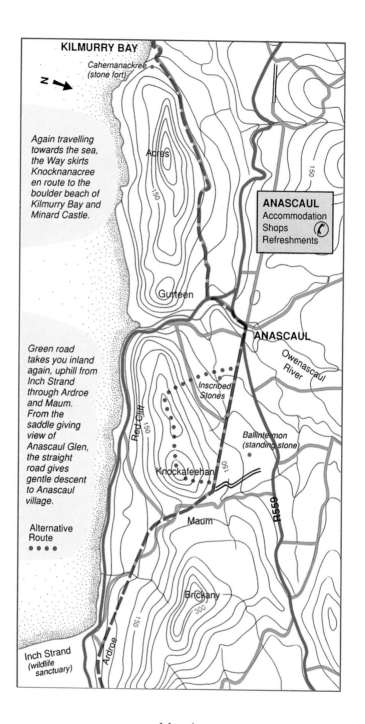

KILMURRY BAY

Cahernanackree
(stone fort)

Again travelling
towards the sea,
the Way skirts
Knocknanacree
en route to the
boulder beach of
Kilmurry Bay and
Minard Castle.

Acres

ANASCAUL
Accommodation
Shops
Refreshments

Gurteen

ANASCAUL

Owenascaul River

Green road
takes you inland
again, uphill from
Inch Strand
through Ardroe
and Maum.
From the
saddle giving
view of
Anascaul Glen,
the straight
road gives
gentle descent
to Anascaul
village.

Inscribed
Stones

Red Cliff

Ballintemon
(standing stone)

R559

Knockafeehan

Alternative
Route
● ● ● ●

Maum

Brickany

Inch Strand
(wildlife
sanctuary)

Ardroe

Map 4

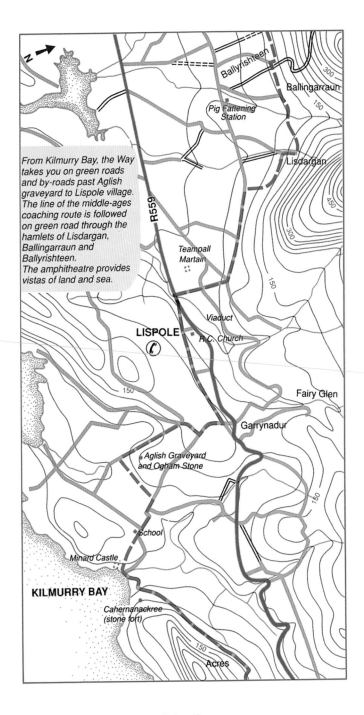

From Kilmurry Bay, the Way takes you on green roads and by-roads past Aglish graveyard to Lispole village. The line of the middle-ages coaching route is followed on green road through the hamlets of Lisdargan, Ballingarraun and Ballyrishteen. The amphitheatre provides vistas of land and sea.

Ballyrishteen

Ballingarraun

Pig Fattening Station

Lisdargan

R559

Teampall Martain

Viaduct

LISPOLE

R.C. Church

Fairy Glen

Garrynadur

Aglish Graveyard and Ogham Stone

School

Minard Castle

KILMURRY BAY

Cahernanackree (stone fort)

Acres

300

150

450

300

150

150

150

150

Map 5

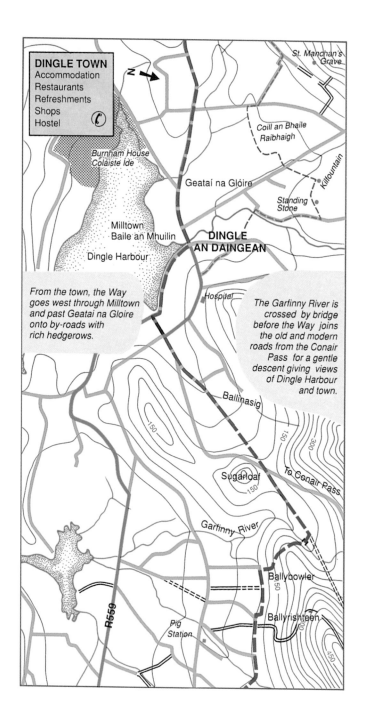

DINGLE TOWN
Accommodation
Restaurants
Refreshments
Shops
Hostel

St. Manchan's Grave

Coill an Bhaile Raibhaigh

Kilfountain

Burnham House
Colaiste Ide

Geataí na Glóire

Standing Stone

Milltown
Baile an Mhuilin

**DINGLE
AN DAINGEAN**

Dingle Harbour

From the town, the Way goes west through Milltown and past Geataí na Glóire onto by-roads with rich hedgerows.

Hospital

The Garfinny River is crossed by bridge before the Way joins the old and modern roads from the Conair Pass for a gentle descent giving views of Dingle Harbour and town.

Ballinasig

To Conair Pass

Sugarloaf

Garfinny River

Ballybowler

Ballyrishteen

R559

Pig Station

Map 6

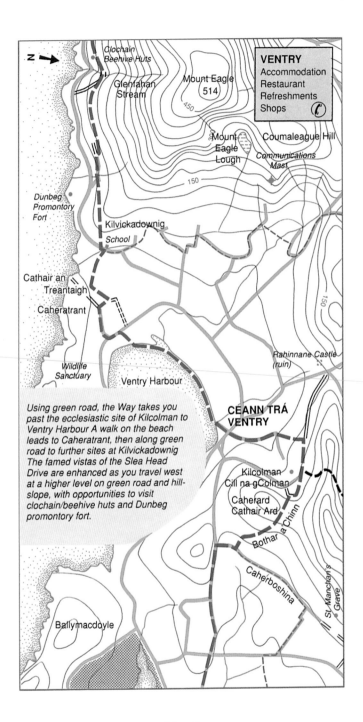

N →

Clochain
Beehive Huts

Glenfahan
Stream

Mount Eagle
514

450

VENTRY
Accommodation
Restaurant
Refreshments
Shops

Mount
Eagle
Lough

Coumaleague Hill

Communications
Mast

150

Dunbeg
Promontory
Fort

Kilvickadownig

School

Cathair an
Treantaigh

Caheratrant

150

Rahinnane Castle
(ruin)

Wildlife
Sanctuary

Ventry Harbour

Using green road, the Way takes you
past the ecclesiastic site of Kilcolman to
Ventry Harbour A walk on the beach
leads to Caheratrant, then along green
road to further sites at Kilvickadownig
The famed vistas of the Slea Head
Drive are enhanced as you travel west
at a higher level on green road and hill-
slope, with opportunities to visit
clochain/beehive huts and Dunbeg
promontory fort.

CEANN TRÁ
VENTRY

Kilcolman
Cill na gColman

Caherard
Cathair Ard

Bothar a Chinn

Caherboshina

St. Manchan's
Grave

Ballymacdoyle

Map 7

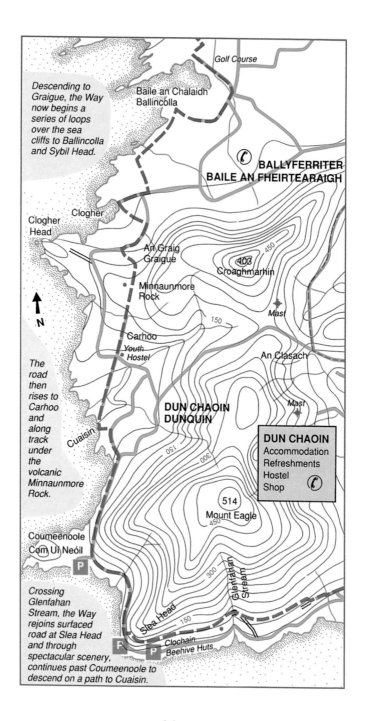

Descending to Graigue, the Way now begins a series of loops over the sea cliffs to Ballincolla and Sybil Head.

Golf Course

Baile an Chalaidh
Ballincolla

BALLYFERRITER
BAILE AN FHEIRTEARAIGH

Clogher
Clogher
Head

An Graig
Graigue

403
Croaghmarhin

450

Minnaunmore
Rock

Mast

150

N

Carhoo
Youth
Hostel

An Clasach

The road then rises to Carhoo and along track under the volcanic Minnaunmore Rock.

Cuaisin

DUN CHAOIN
DUNQUIN

Mast

150

300

DUN CHAOIN
Accommodation
Refreshments
Hostel
Shop

514
Mount Eagle

450

Coumeenoole
Com Uí Neóil

P

300

Glenfahan Stream

Crossing Glenfahan Stream, the Way rejoins surfaced road at Slea Head and through spectacular scenery, continues past Coumeenoole to descend on a path to Cuaisin.

Slea Head

150

P
P

Clochain
Beehive Huts

Map 8

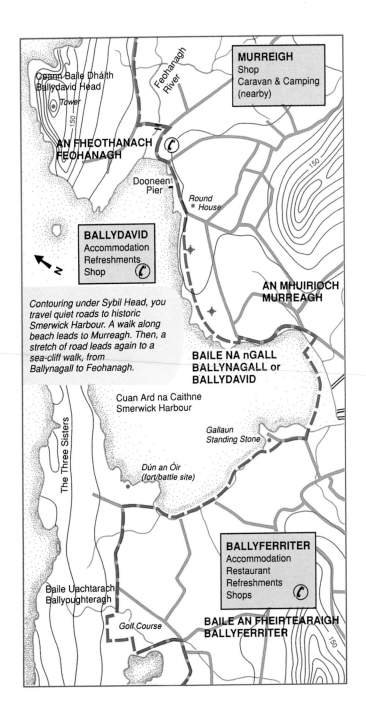

MURREIGH
Shop
Caravan & Camping
(nearby)

Ceann Baile Dháith
Ballydavid Head
Tower

150

**AN FHEOTHANACH
FEOHANAGH**

Feohanagh
River

Dooneen
Pier

*Round
House*

150

BALLYDAVID
Accommodation
Refreshments
Shop

**AN MHUIRIOCH
MURREAGH**

N

*Contouring under Sybil Head, you
travel quiet roads to historic
Smerwick Harbour. A walk along
beach leads to Murreagh. Then, a
stretch of road leads again to a
sea-cliff walk, from
Ballynagall to Feohanagh.*

**BAILE NA nGALL
BALLYNAGALL or
BALLYDAVID**

*Cuan Ard na Caithne
Smerwick Harbour*

The Three Sisters

*Gallaun
Standing Stone*

*Dún an Óir
(fort/battle site)*

BALLYFERRITER
Accommodation
Restaurant
Refreshments
Shops

Baile Uachtarach
Ballyoughteragh

**BAILE AN FHEIRTEARAIGH
BALLYFERRITER**

Golf Course

150

Map 9

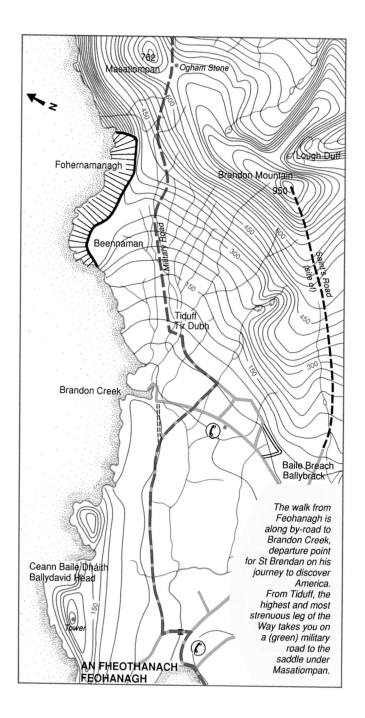

The walk from Feohanagh is along by-road to Brandon Creek, departure point for St Brendan on his journey to discover America. From Tiduff, the highest and most strenuous leg of the Way takes you on a (green) military road to the saddle under Masatiompan.

Map 10

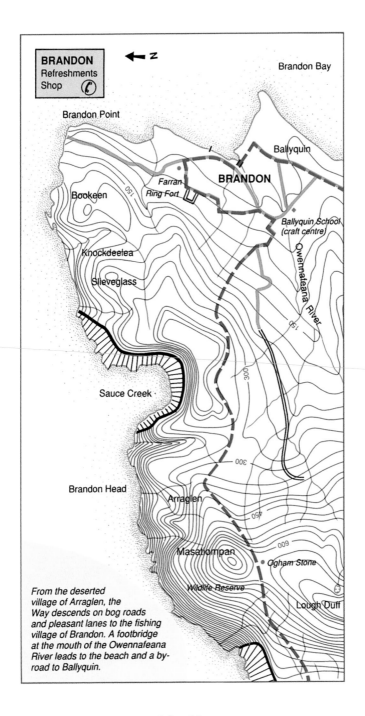

From the deserted village of Arraglen, the Way descends on bog roads and pleasant lanes to the fishing village of Brandon. A footbridge at the mouth of the Owennafeana River leads to the beach and a by-road to Ballyquin.

Map 11

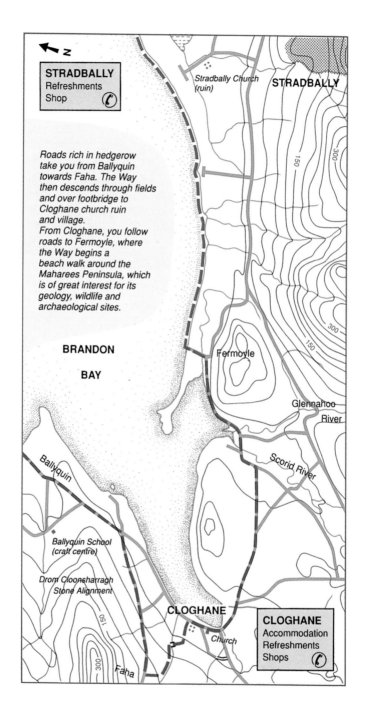

STRADBALLY
Refreshments
Shop

Roads rich in hedgerow take you from Ballyquin towards Faha. The Way then descends through fields and over footbridge to Cloghane church ruin and village.
From Cloghane, you follow roads to Fermoyle, where the Way begins a beach walk around the Maharees Peninsula, which is of great interest for its geology, wildlife and archaeological sites.

Stradbally Church (ruin)

STRADBALLY

BRANDON

BAY

Fermoyle

Glennahoo River

Scorid River

Ballyquin

Ballyquin School (craft centre)

Drom Cloonsharragh Stone Alignment

CLOGHANE

Church

CLOGHANE
Accommodation
Refreshments
Shops

Faha

Map 12

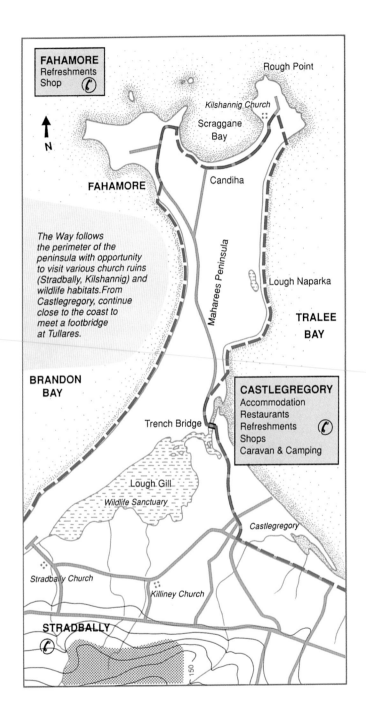

FAHAMORE
Refreshments
Shop

Rough Point

Kilshannig Church

Scraggane
Bay

N

FAHAMORE

Candiha

*The Way follows
the perimeter of the
peninsula with opportunity
to visit various church ruins
(Stradbally, Kilshannig) and
wildlife habitats.From
Castlegregory, continue
close to the coast to
meet a footbridge
at Tullares.*

Maharees Peninsula

Lough Naparka

**TRALEE
BAY**

**BRANDON
BAY**

Trench Bridge

CASTLEGREGORY
Accommodation
Restaurants
Refreshments
Shops
Caravan & Camping

Lough Gill
Wildlife Sanctuary

Castlegregory

Stradbally Church

Killiney Church

STRADBALLY

150

Map 13

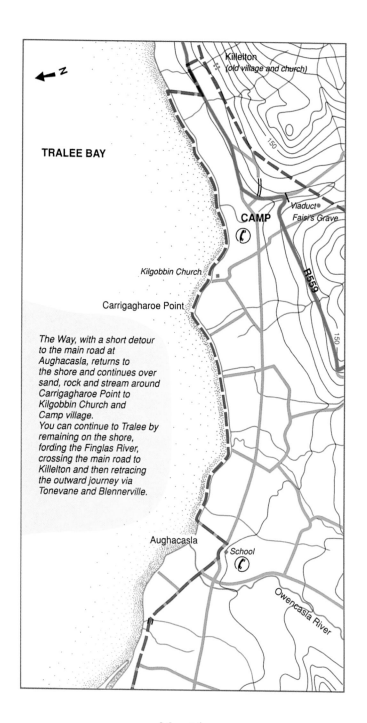

N ←

TRALEE BAY

Killelton
(old village and church)

150

Viaduct
Faisi's Grave

CAMP

R559

150

Kilgobbin Church

Carrigagharoe Point

*The Way, with a short detour
to the main road at
Aughacasla, returns to
the shore and continues over
sand, rock and stream around
Carrigagharoe Point to
Kilgobbin Church and
Camp village.
You can continue to Tralee by
remaining on the shore,
fording the Finglas River,
crossing the main road to
Killelton and then retracing
the outward journey via
Tonevane and Blennerville.*

Aughacasla

School

Owencasla River

Map 14

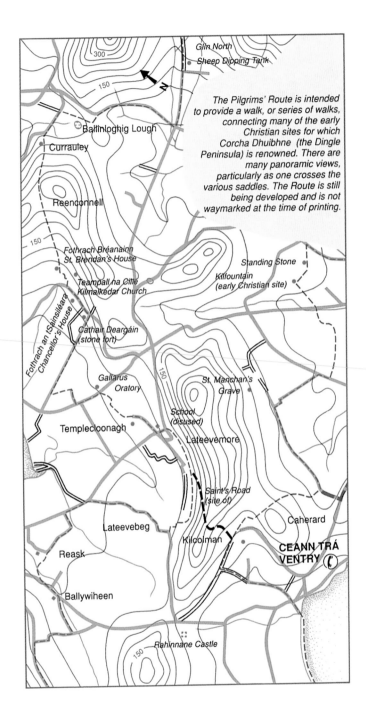

The Pilgrims' Route is intended to provide a walk, or series of walks, connecting many of the early Christian sites for which Corcha Dhuibhne (the Dingle Peninsula) is renowned. There are many panoramic views, particularly as one crosses the various saddles. The Route is still being developed and is not waymarked at the time of printing.

Map 15

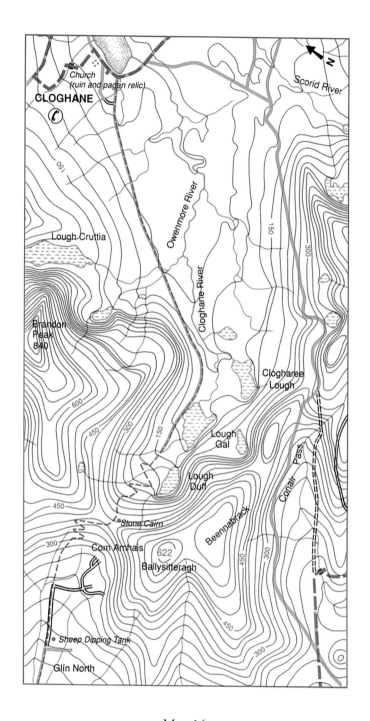

Map 16

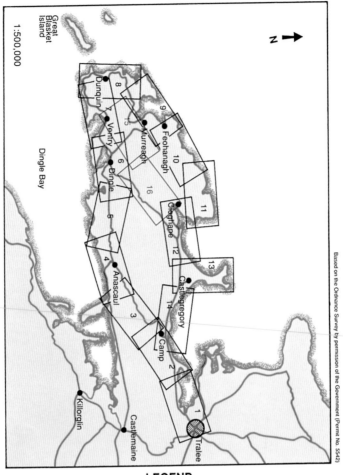

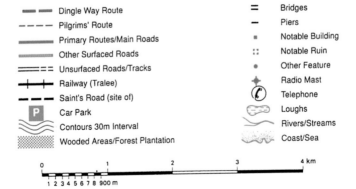

LEGEND

— — Dingle Way Route	= Bridges
---- Pilgrims' Route	— Piers
—— Primary Routes/Main Roads	▪ Notable Building
—— Other Surfaced Roads	∷ Notable Ruin
≡≡≡ Unsurfaced Roads/Tracks	● Other Feature
┼┼┼ Railway (Tralee)	Radio Mast
— — Saint's Road (site of)	Telephone
P Car Park	Loughs
Contours 30m Interval	Rivers/Streams
Wooded Areas/Forest Plantation	Coast/Sea

IRISH WORDS IN PLACENAMES

Irish	Anglicised form	English
Abha, abhainn	ow, owen	river
Achadh	agha, augh	field
Árd		height
Baile	bally	townland
Bán	bawn	white
Barr		top
Beag	beg	small
Béal		mouth
Bearna	barna	gap
Binn	ben	peak
Bóthar	boher	road
Bótharín	bohareen, boreen	small road
Breac	brack	speckled
Carraig	carrig	rock
Cathair	caher	stone fort
Ceann	ken	head (land)
Cill	kill	church
Clár	clare	expanse of land
Cloch		stone
Cluain	cloon	meadow
Cnoc	knock	hill
Coill	kyle	wood
Cruach	croagh	steep hill
Com	coum	corrie, cirque
Dearg	darrig	red
Doire	derry	oak-wood
Droim	drum	ridge
Dubh	duff	black
Dún	doon	fort
Eas	ass	waterfall

Eisc	eask, esk	cliff
Faiche	faha	green, lawn
Faill, aill	foil	cliff
Fionn	fin, ven	white, bright
Gaoith	gwee	wind
Glas	glass	green
Glas	glash	stream
Gleann	glen	valley
Gort		field
Imeallach	emlagh	marginal land
Inis	inish	island
Leac	lack	flagstone
Leaca, leacan	lacken	hillside
Lios	lis	ring fort
Loch	lough	lake
Lug, lag		hollow
Má		plain
Macha	magha	cattle-field
Mám	maum	pass
Maol		bare
Más		buttock
Mór	more	big
Mullach	mullagh	summit
Oileán	illaun	island
Ráth		ringfort
Rinn	reen	point
Rua	roe	red
Sceilig	skellig	rock
Sean	shan	old
Sliabh	slieve	mountain
Taobh	teeve	side
Tír	teer	land
Teach		house
Tobar	tubber	well
Tor		tall rock
Trá		strand
Tulach	tullig	low hill

INDEX

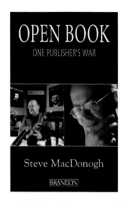

Steve MacDonogh

Open Book: One Publisher's War

"MacDonogh is without doubt the most adventurous and determined of the Irish publishers . . . This is an important book." *Phoenix*

"A fascinating and very important book." *Brid Rosney, Today FM*

"The parallels between Orwell and MacDonogh are striking . . . MacDonogh's transparent writing is redolent of Orwell's famous 'plain style'. Most significant of all, . . . Orwell believed that the fate of democracy is linked with that of literature. MacDonogh's career is an illustration of that point . . . *Open Book* is an intelligent, informative account of a life spent fighting for freedom of speech, a right which is still not adequately safeguarded." *Irish World*

"Fascinating reading." *Sunday Business Post*

Paperback £8.99   ISBN 0 86322 263 3

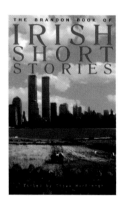

Steve MacDonogh (ed)

The Brandon Book of Irish Short Stories

"The confident internationalism of these mostly young writers reflects something of the spirit of the new Ireland but it is grounded in an undeceived realism . . . On the evidence here, the future of Irish fiction is in good hands." *Observer*

"This impressive collection." *Times Literary Supplement*

"Stories illuminating experiences and emotions that are universal and instantly familiar . . . The book is also excellent value for money." *Examiner*

"A host of the best contemporary Irish writers." *Ireland on Sunday*

"This exciting collection of short fiction by twenty-three new and newish Irish writers transcends geographic and psychological boundaries." *The Irish Times*

Paperback £6.99   ISBN 0 86322 237 4

Available from good bookshops and from

Brandon/Mount Eagle Publications
P.O. Box 32
Dingle, Co. Kerry, Ireland